THE
LAST
SEVEN
DAYS

McDougal & Associates

Servants of Christ and Stewards of the
Mysteries of God

THE
LAST
SEVEN
DAYS

THE HEALING AND PURGING PATH OF
GOD FOR THE LAST DAYS ON EARTH

By

T.W. Barkley

Published by:

McDougal & Associates
18896 Greenwell Springs Road
Greenwell Springs, Louisiana 70739
www.thepublishedword.com

McDougal & Associates is an organization dedicated to the spreading the Gospel of the Lord Jesus Christ to as many people as possible in the shortest time possible.

ISBN: 978-1-940461-61-8

Printed on Demand in the U.S., the U.K. and Australia
For Worldwide Distribution

DEDICATION

I dedicate this book to my three sons: Terzeno, Thomas and Timothy Barkley. I am so proud of you guys' strength and love and how you overcame all of the challenges of life coming up.

I especially want to dedicate this book to my grandson "Fatdaddy" and all my other grandchildren.

SPECIAL THANKS

I would like to thank Sisters Stephanay Manley, Debra Hill, Katrina Morten and Minister Harriet Hilliard for helping to sustain the vision during the writing of this book.

Very special thanks to my Senior Administrator Linda Wang for supporting and helping me with the proofing and editing to make the book a reality.

CONTENTS

Behold, I have refined thee, but not with silver;
I have chosen thee in the furnace of affliction.
Isaiah 10:48

PREFACE

GOD IS PURGING US TODAY SO THAT WE CAN ESCAPE HIS FINAL PURGE

The Last Seven Days ... God's elect are those of this generation who will overcome the end-time trials and the judgment of God and will also hear an end-time sound. That sound will help lead them to safety and victory in this life and in the new world to come.

The temperature gets hotter and hotter each day. The sky is goldish black. Air-conditioning units, cars and all other (of what have become to us) "life necessities" are breaking down. People are running in the streets. Their bodies are hot and being scorched, and they are diving into the dirt and rolling about on the ground, trying to cool off.

The rivers are also burning, actually catching on fire. The water in them is so hot. The streets are hot. Homes are hot. Entire city blocks of homes are sinking into the ground as sinkholes are spreading throughout entire communities. People are running to their cars, trying to get away, but their cars are too hot to touch. Others are stampeding in crowds down the streets. John 15:2 declares:

Every branch in me that beareth not fruit he taketh away: and every branch that beareth fruit, he purgeth it, that it may bring forth more fruit.

God is purging us today so that we may escape the final purge on Earth tomorrow. It is my desire that this book will prepare you and an entire generation for the bone-chilling never-before-heard-of coming events.

Today so many believers are blaming and crediting Satan for some of the things God is working out of them. It is often hard for us to understand that the crises and challenges we often experience are, in reality, God's love at work trying to purge us from sin and from satanic strongholds.

This book is a culmination of things I have seen in visions and dreams and should be used as a training manual. It is a prophetic voice and direction, a tool to help you understand God's purging process for total obedience for your healing and deliverance and for your heavenly-bound journey. You will never be the same after I take you into the world of my visions. You will see with me the purging rooms, and, finally, my prophetic glimpse into *The Last Seven Days* on Earth.

Tommie Barkley
Houston, Texas

Part 1

My Visions of the Last Days

CHAPTER 1

THE MYSTERY OF GOD, THE GIFT AND EVIL IN THE WORLD

I form the light, and create darkness: I make peace, and create evil: I the LORD do all these things.

Isaiah 45:7

God created everything, good and evil. In today's society, people, among them many Christians, blame God for the bad things that happen in the world. Ministers today often say, "Give God something to work with," as they cite Mark 6:41, where the disciples of Jesus took five loaves and two fish from a young lad and handed them to Him. After He had prayed over the loaves, they were multiplied to feed five thousand people.

In the same way, after Adam and Eve sinned, we gave God sin to work with. We did not know evil in the beginning. Evil only came upon mankind because of man's disobedience to God in the Garden. It had not existed before that. Sin was dormant until Satan activated it to destroy us, but God used it to save us instead.

In the Old Testament, God had to work with sin and, through sin, to get us to Heaven:

And there came forth a spirit, and stood before the LORD, and said, I will persuade him.
And the LORD said unto him, Wherewith?
And he said, I will go forth, and I will be a lying spirit in the mouth of all his prophets.
And he said, Thou shalt persuade him, and prevail also: go forth, and do so.
Now therefore, behold, the LORD hath put a lying spirit in the mouth of all these prophets, and the LORD hath spoken evil concerning thee. 1 Kings 22:21-23

And it came to pass, when the evil spirit from God was upon Saul that David took an harp, and played with his hand: so Saul was refreshed, and was well, and the evil spirit departed from him.
1 Samuel 16:23

Jesus Christ, the Spirit of Truth, who was to prove a *"more perfect way,"* had not yet come:

Howbeit when he, the Spirit of truth, is come, he will guide you into all truth: for he shall not speak of himself; but whatsoever he shall hear, that shall he speak: and he will shew you things to come. John 16:13

THE GIFT

It is my firm belief that God has given us a gift that will be the major player in the end-times. I believe that this gift will guide us to the Promised Land during the end-times and keep us from the coming judgement. I believe that only those who are active in praying with and obeying this gift will be matured enough to follow it's leading.

I believe that this Gift is the most misunderstood and best kept secret around today. To all who read this book, I am referring to the presence of the Holy Spirit or the baptism and gift of the Holy Ghost, as taught in the Word of God. My own personal Texas way of saying it is this: have you gotten your portion of the presence and power of God?

In recent centuries this gift was only embraced by the classical Pentecostals, but today it is being embraced by major denominations around the world, including Catholics, Methodists, Lutherans, Presbyterians and Baptists. The reason major religious groups have come to trust this experience is that they now have proof that individuals who have had the experience have an astounding amount of joy and peace, along with more victorious testimonies after they have received it.

Many receive supernatural miracles and healings during their initial infilling and operate in signs and wonders afterward. They also tend to live longer and seem to be stronger when facing the spiritual battles of life.

Do not the Scriptures teach?

While Peter was still speaking these words, the Holy
Spirit fell upon all those who were listening to the
message. All the circumcised believers who came
with Peter were amazed, because the gift of the Holy
Spirit had been poured out on the Gentiles also.
Acts 10:44-45, NASB

Peter said to them, "Repent, and each of you be
baptized in the name of Jesus Christ for the forgive-
ness of your sins; and you will receive the gift of
the Holy Spirit. For the promise is for you and your
children and for all who are far off, as many as the
Lord our God will call to Himself."
Acts 2:38-39, NASB

God is looking for yielded vessels. It wasn't long after being called into ministry that I started operating in what I called "my mother's anointing" to deal with demon spirits. I remember one day as I had just lain down in bed, getting ready to relax and watch some television, I got a page on my pager. It was from my good friend Evangelist Greg Griffen. It seemed that he was in a revival at a local Baptist church and had encountered a precious woman who was totally demonized through witchcraft. He was requesting my help, so I immediately got up and made my way to that church.

When I arrived at the Baptist church, the ushers were waiting for me at the door. After confirming my name, they took me immediately up to the platform. Brother Griffen briefed me on the details and released me to minister to the woman.

As I approached this woman, she tried to fool me, by acting very innocent. When I didn't buy it, she started making different faces and tried to trance me with her sexy body. After that didn't work, she tried to frighten me. Within fifteen minutes, it was all over as I laid hands on her and cast out the demon. Her eyes rolled to the back of her head, and she started sobbing and moaning as the spirit left her. Afterward, the other people present began to clap as I hurriedly made my way out the door and to my car.

Many times pastors called me this way, with cold calls for deliverance, and each time God was faithful. It was all done in faith in the name of Jesus. God uses His people with the gift to deliver men and women from evil.

THE MYSTERY OF THE THREE HEAVENS REVEALED

During the early years of my ministry, while I was on a long fast, the Lord visited me and gave me this revelation concerning the three different heavens. Genesis 1:1 states that God created *"the heavens"*—plural. In 2 Corinthians 12:2, the apostle Paul states, *"I knew a man in Christ above fourteen years ago, (whether in the body, I cannot tell; or whether out of the body, I cannot tell: God knoweth;) such an one caught up to the third heaven."*

The 3rd Heaven: Is the place where God and His heavenly hosts live, where the throne of God is. This is the place where there is no evil or wickedness, nor can anything wicked ever be there. Referred to as *"the heaven of heavens"* by Nehemiah (see Nehemiah 9:6). It is referenced in

Revelation 21:27: *"And there shall in no wise enter into it any-thing that defileth, neither whatsoever worketh abomination, or maketh a lie: but they which are written in the Lamb's book of life.*

The 2nd Heaven: Is the place or spiritual realm where demonic battles are fought and spiritual warfare takes place. The entrance to this heaven is through our minds. Job 1:6 says, *"Now there was a day when the sons of God came to present themselves before the LORD, and Satan came also among them."* We can see here that Satan had access to God to come before Him and accuse the brethren. Even today Satan has that same access, according to Luke 22:31-32. It says, *"Simon, Simon, behold, Satan hath desired to have you, that he may sift you as wheat: but I have prayed for thee that thy faith fail the not: and when thou art converted, strengthen thy brethren."* Satan still communicates with the Almighty.

In Matthew 6:10, *"Thy kingdom come, Thy will be done in earth, as it is in heaven,"* we get a clue about bringing victory into our circumstances today as we bring the Kingdom of Heaven into our world and life.

Here are a few scriptures I hope will help you to access this place through your mind. Philippians 2:5: *"Let this mind be in you, which was also in Christ Jesus."* 2 Corinthians 10:3-5: *"For though we walk in the flesh, we do not war after the flesh: (for the weapons of our warfare are not carnal, but mighty through God to the pulling down of strong holds;) casting down imaginations, and every high thing that exalteth itself against the knowledge of God, and bringing into captivity every thought to the obedience of Christ."*

The 1st Heaven: If we parallel the three heavens to our body (the 1st heaven), soul (the 2nd heaven) and spirit (the

3rd heaven), we can easily understand the 1st heaven is all that we can see in the earth and in the air around the earth. It is this heaven and the 2nd heaven that will be destroyed on that great day. Revelation 21:1-2: *"And I saw a new heaven and a new earth: for the first heaven and the first earth were passed away; and there was no more sea. And I John saw the holy city, new Jerusalem, coming down from God out of heaven, prepared as a bride adorned for her husband."*

CHAPTER 2

MY VISION OF THE END

All through my dreams one night I kept hearing the word *resonance*. As this word *resonance* rang out in my spirit, powerful events would happen. Resonance people were going to homes to feed the hungry and suffering and help them with their bills and other crises. Resonance people were getting out of wheelchairs in revivals. Resonance people were finding favor with bills and house notes and supernaturally receiving financial blessings and blessed relationships by the Holy Spirit. Resonance gangs were experiencing the power of God.

Resonance was birthing a true revival in which miraculous feats were happening.

Resonance people were experiencing salvation in the prisons, streets and hospitals, on buses and in schools. Even news networks were talking about an unprecedented supernatural movement in the land.

As I studied the etymology of the word *resonance*, I came up with the resounding fact that resonance is "a reverberating sound, an echo." *Miriam Webster's Dictionary* says it is "the quality of a sound that stays loud, clear and deep for a long time; a quality that makes something personally meaningful or important to someone."

In one of my visions, there was a certain house where a white couple was sleeping. They were awakened by a rushing, mighty wind horn sound coming from within them. (No one else could hear it.) Their hands were shaking as if they were in a Pentecostal worship service.

A white middle-aged couple, Jim and Laura, were rising up from bed quietly but quickly and then dressing in a hurry. They were packing clothes into a suitcase and looking around bewildered. Laura asked, "Honey, how many days are we packing for?"

Jim answered her, "Seven days at least."

Laura sighed, "Okay."

They looked around the room, but only their eyes were moving. Then, calmly and in a brave, confident manner, they quickly left.

I saw a vision of urban Houston. An African-American couple, E.J. and Gloria Oday, were pulling up outside their apartment and getting out of their car They were making small talk, after spending a great night out. Then, however, they heard bells with a rushing wind sound from within.

The image of a shadow was seen on their bodies, and their hands shook as if they were in a Pentecostal worship service. They hastily went inside to pack their belongings.

I heard E.J. say, "Come on, Baby, get the kids and let's go!" When she didn't move fast enough to suit him, he said more forcefully, "Go! Go!"

"Okay, Baby," she replied.

She hurried into the bedroom of two teenager girls and a seven-year-old boy. They were all asleep, but she woke them up. Then, there was no sound, just silence, as they all got up and began to pack their clothes.

They all left the house in a slow-motion scene with just a few suitcases. As they headed to the car, the wind and horn sound was heard again. Others who were walking by could not hear what they were hearing.

That same night I saw two young adults, Lenora Ortega, a news lady who was coming out of an airport talking to her cameraman, Raymond Hernandez. He carried a camera in one hand as they walked toward their vehicle. Lenora said, "It's been a long week. I'll see you at church on Sunday."

Then, however, as they unloaded their gear into the back of the SUV, their eyes locked. They were in love but were fighting it. Raymond said, "Will you have a late night brunch with me?"

They looked at each other and laughed, and then both said at the same time: "Yes!"

But, before they could say anything else, they heard the same chime sound coming from within, and their hands began to shake as well (the classic Pentecostal shake when God's presence is felt).

Raymond hurriedly backed the SUV out and took off. After driving only a few minutes, they came to a dark road and a huge seven-sided building with a beautiful glow and bluish mist around it. They were overwhelmed with the presence of this beautiful building and were struggling with the fact that they had never noticed it before. It seemed that there was a force that mysteriously drew them to it now.

Outside of the huge seven-sided building, the moon was full and casting a tint into the night, creating an eerie look in the sky. Other cars drove up, and other couples, along with Raymond and Lenora, were meeting and greeting each other, as they went into the seven-sided building. Other people present at this meeting were Doctor Mei Li Cheng, Officer Pendleton and Isabel Love.

The sky lit up with lightning, and the thunder clapped. Across the street from the seven-sided building there was a small stream of smoke coming up from the ground, and there was a shadow of an image that was traveling up and down. It also traveled to the bottom of the Earth. The image met another shadow, or silhouette, that was still and not moving. Then, suddenly, the sounds of a fire were heard, and the images made a quick move out of sight.

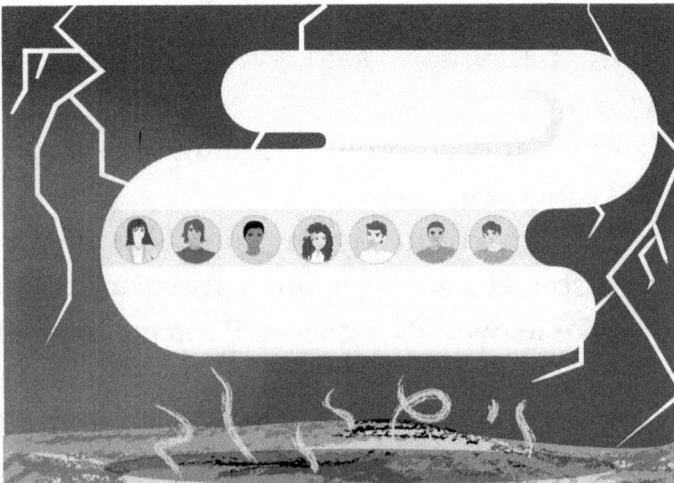

That same night, at the huge seven-sided building, I saw that it was tall and strong, made with what looked like bronze. The wind was blowing around it, and seven light beams were shining down on the seven corners of the building, reflecting off of the glass windows on various floors. The bluish tint was so beautiful. There was only one road that led to this building, and it was protected by glass walls.

There were people on various floors of this tall building. Some of the rooms were labelled "Surgery." These rooms were revealed to me as purging rooms, and other rooms as vision rooms. There were seven purging rooms on each floor, and each room was named after a specific demon category mentioned in the New Testament. These room names were:

1. Evil Spirit
2. Fear Spirit
3. Unclean Spirit
4. Infirm Spirit
5. Deaf and Dumb Spirit
6. Divination Spirit and
7. Seducing Spirit

(I will share later the people who went into each of these rooms for help.)

There were incredible-looking animals, including frogs, cat-like looking leopards, and a breed of dogs I had never seen before. There were also snakes, bulls, goats and others, and they were scaling straight up the walls of the building. It seemed that these were demon spirits that were trying to take hold of the people in the purging rooms.

As the people were cleansed from their demonic influences, the spirits were tossed outside and landed on the outer walls of the building. At certain times, you could hear loud-sounding chains turning and grinding, as the building would lift up off of the ground and spin to the next of the seven sides and then drop back to the ground, knocking off the animals and all the little insects that were on it in the process. Then a hot vapor would clean it and dry it.

CHAPTER 3

MY VISION OF THE PURGING ROOMS

For my name's sake will I defer mine anger, and for my praise will I refrain for thee, that I cut thee not off. Behold, I have refined thee, but not with silver; I have chosen thee in the furnace of affliction. For mine own sake, even for mine own sake, will I do it: for how should my name be polluted? and I will not give my glory unto another.   Isaiah 48:9-11

One thing that stuck out to me from my visions was the fact that only ten percent of the television ministers and ten percent of American pastors and ministers made it into and through the purging rooms and remained faithful to God and His message. The rest were destroyed by fire.

When a minster would go into one of the purging rooms, a very weird and noisy sound was heard. The rooms had balances, and if the floor in the room tilted to the left, those inside were being warned about being a weak and fearful leader, compromising the Word and preaching messages to please the people. The ministers were warned loudly that God would not know them if they persisted. If the floor in the room tilted to the right, they were warned about being too self-righteous and prideful.

Ninety percent of the ministers and eighty percent of the people did not want to deal with the purging rooms. They not only left the rooms; they eventually left the building and went back outside. Many of these would later be met by the fire of destruction. The rest of us were promoted in a special ceremony and sent to the top of the building.

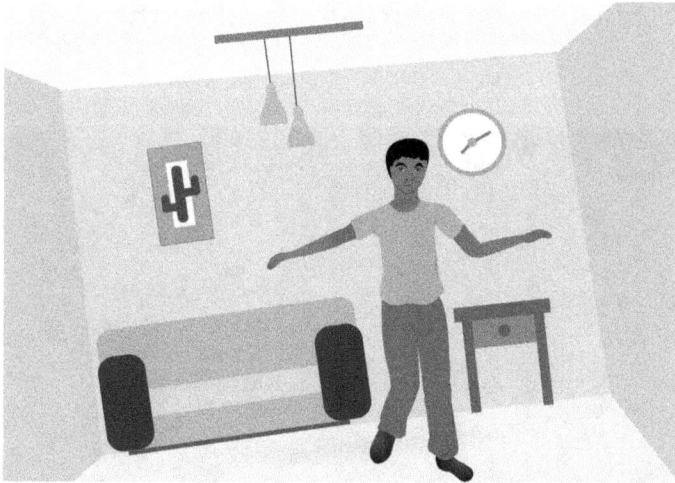

When we got to the top of the building there was a beautiful wind sound accompanied by golden, purple and blue vapors. It was very beautiful.

There were two angels that guided us to one of four big bullet-looking trains. These trains were huge and strong-looking, with powerful iron sides and beautiful big wings on each side. We heard a loud voice over us saying, "Last call to rest for salvation on Earth!" Then the trains slowly took off, blowing a powerful-sounding horn (the four winds).

We all got into position on each side of the train, and each of us had a window to lean out of and were able to pull people from outside (literally snatching them into the Glory Train). There were all kinds of people on the train—family members, friends, former convicts, factory workers, professional and white collar workers, athletes and former gays who had found salvation, along with many ministers. As the train roared around the world, we saw all kinds of miracles happening. Because people were suffering from wars, famine and natural disasters, they were getting on the train. But many people rejected us and continued on in their lifestyles. Some even came against the train and tried to stop it.

As the train proceeded, everyone was pulling people in, and all sorts of people were being rescued. As the horn blasted, we continued bringing people in as fast as we could.

There were earthquakes in places that had never seen one before. I remember seeing news reports of entire city blocks being swallowed up as the ground opened mysteriously in random locations.

Finally, the train got to a point where it came to a stop, and we heard the words "Last Stop!" Everything was so quiet in that place. We all relaxed a little when we were told that this last stop was, again, for family and friends and also for personal visits. It was 12:01 AM midnight, and we were told that we were being allowed seven hours to go and get as many people as we could.

Most of us got off the train, to go to a store or to call family members and friends, urging them to get on with us.

As I was coming back to the big train that next morning, I was a little late. I saw many people getting on, and I heard the horn sound, and the train started moving. I, along with others who were also late, fearfully ran to catch the train.

I started crying out to the Lord, "Please don't leave me!" Others cried out too. Then I ran! I ran harder than I'd ever run before. I caught up to the train, and someone snatched me back inside. I was so happy and thankful.

Eventually the train slowed and went into an S-like curve, and I heard the wheels grinding on the tracks. The horn blew so loud we had to cover our ears. Then the train came to a halt for the final time.

I heard and saw a beautiful wind swirling around the train, accompanied by golden, purple and blue vapors. It was so beautiful. Then a voice came through the air and told us to pray.

As we all began to pray, we heard several men and women screaming. We looked over at them and were surprised to see the wind literally sucking them out of the train into the air and then hurling them back to the ground outside. The voice came back on the air, as we sat speechless, wondering what had just happened.

The voice came again and quoted Matthew:

For there shall arise false Christs, and false prophets, and shall shew great signs and wonders; insomuch that, if it were possible, they shall deceive the very elect. Matthew 24:24

Then, as I sat there, I heard and saw the windows and doors locking one at a time. It was a shocking feeling.

Click!
Click!
Click!
Bam!
Bam!
Bam!

The windows were closing, and the doors were locking all throughout the huge train.

Then there were two angels that said, "Well done!" and instructed us about the New Heaven and New Earth. It seemed that the swirling wind was also sort of a force field. We asked about the wind and were told the train was sealed and, from this point on, no one could get out of it, and no one could get into it.

We were all looking out the window at our communities, and eventually we all looked up to Heaven. Everything was so quiet.

Then we heard the sound of a lifetime. The train, with steam coming out its sides, suddenly blasted upward like a rocket from a launch pad. It blasted straight up through the clouds, with the cars firmly in a straight line, as if there were an invisible track in the sky.

CHAPTER 4

MY VISION OF THE FOUR WINDS

The train finally arrived back at the huge building from where it had originally departed, and I heard the windows and doors unlocking one by one.

Click!

Click!

Click!

Bam!

Bam!

Bam!

After that, we were all assembled inside the huge seven-cornered building and were told to be seated. And we were again told, "Well done!"

Then the same thing that had happened on the train happened again, this time in the building. All of the windows and doors began locking, even as the beautiful wind swirled around the building. It was amazing!

I looked out the window and saw three more buildings with the wind swirling around them across the skyline. That was when the scripture came to me from Matthew:

And he shall send his angels with a great sound of a trumpet, and they shall gather together his elect from the four winds, from one end of heaven to the other.
                                                    Matthew 24:31

Now, when we looked out the windows, we could see around the world.

I looked around inside the big room we were all in (we were with those we had picked up on the train). Everyone was having so much fun, and it was very peaceful. Everyone was very happy, laughing, walking around and meeting others. It was as if I was the only one who could see the events of the world.

A little later, I felt the huge building move and hover over the ground about a thousand feet up. Then the words JESUS IS LORD shined forth from the building.

The whole Earth was pitch black; there was no sun and no moon. The only thing that had light was the huge building I was in and the three other buildings in the air.

As we hovered in one spot over the ground, I began to see and hear the following: the whole world screaming and crying. People were screaming, trying to get into the huge building we were in. They were jumping off walls, trying to get into planes and helicopters. These aircraft were circling, trying to get in, but they could not and eventually crashed from the heat.

There were all kinds of people: gay couples, ministers, political leaders, gang leaders and others, all begging God to let them in. As they slowly succumbed to the heat and fire, they were chanting and screaming in unison, "Jesus is Lord!" Too late they had come to realize the truth.

People were dropping to their knees with their hands lifted up and were literally burning, with the sizzling sound of fire, like wood crackling, trying to get into the building.

There were also demon spirits coming up from the ground that would wrap themselves around people who were running and screaming, and the demons would literally ignite into a flame of fire so that the people seemed like running balls of fire.

The sound of their screams was terrifying. Others were being burned by the stars as they fell to Earth. The heat from them alone was killing many. There was fire everywhere, and it could not be stopped. All of what we now consider "life's necessities" were breaking down.

People were running in the streets naked, as their bodies were hot and scorched. They were diving into the dirt and rolling on the ground, trying to cool off. The rivers were catching on fire because the water was so hot. The streets were hot. Homes were hot. Entire city blocks of homes were sinking below the ground as sinkholes spread throughout entire communities.

People were running to their cars, trying to get away, but their cars were too hot to touch. Others were stampeding in crowds down the streets. But all the roads and streets were crumbling, and there was no more level ground, only deep, dark terrain, and the people could no longer see where to go. The Bible declares:

Whereby the world that then was, being overflowed with water, perished: but the heavens and the earth, which are now, by the same word are kept in store, reserved unto fire against the day of judgment and perdition of ungodly men. 2 Peter 3:6-7

The Lord is not slack concerning His promise, as some count slackness, but is longsuffering toward us, not willing that any should perish but that all should come to repentance. But the day of the Lord will come as a thief in the night, in which the heavens will pass away with a great noise, and the elements will melt with fervent heat; both the earth and the works that are in it will be burned up. Therefore, since all these things shall be dissolved, what manner of persons ought you to be in holy conduct and godliness? 2 Peter 9:10-11

It was happening.

Part II

The Preparation

CHAPTER 5

HOW IT ALL STARTED

In 1961, when I was just eight, I was out of the street one night, in the busy crime-ridden area of Houston's notorious Third Ward. A thief was running out of a nearby store with some stolen merchandise and being chased by the attendant. I heard sirens and saw prostitutes working the corners. Pimps and drug dealers drove slowly by, and I saw a barefooted drunk in a notorious alley, trying to sell his shoes to buy more liquor.

Standing on the corner of Dowling and Holman, I was talking to a prostitute. She had asked me to get her a soda, and I was bringing her the change. "Keep the change, little man," she said.

Pointing to her breasts, I said, "Tell you what ... Why don't you let me touch those things?"

"What?" she asked, feigning alarm. "Little man, your mama and daddy know you on this corner?"

Just then a pimp known as Daddy Z drove up, jumped out of his car and began yelling at the prostitute. She (and the rest of the neighborhood people) were all afraid of Daddy Z. He was bad business.

I heard him demanding of her, "Where's my money?" And then he said, "And I heard you were late?"

This woman had been kind to me. Sensing that she was in trouble, I chimed in, "Hey, man, the pigs had her, asking her questions. And, besides, you ain't nothin but a chump with an old raggedy lac. Look at ya old punk car!"

Daddy Z looked at the prostitute with a mean face and asked her, "Is that true?"

The prostitute answered, "Daddy Z, that's the real deal, Baby!"

Then, the pimp turned, looked directly at me and made a threatening gesture as if he was going to hit me. I ran to get out of his reach.

Soon Daddy Z got in his car, looked my way and rolled his eyes, trying to scare me. Then, as he was driving off, he called out, "Little old popeyed joker, get somewhere!"

Once Daddy Z was out of the way, the prostitute turned toward me. It was obvious that she was thankful I had lied for her. Without a word, she took my hand and put it on her big breast, and said, "Don't ever buy it. That makes you a trick, okay? And once a trick for a woman, you will always be a trick to that woman."

Smiling and shaking my head in agreement, I said, "Okay" and wandered on home.

I should have known better. My mother had grown up in Pentecostal circles and had taken us to church from the time we were infants. We heard the Bible preached every week. I think what emboldened me on that street corner was that I had always known I was to be a Moses type, helping others as I did that prostitute.

As a child, I suffered terribly from asthma attacks. One day I was home sick, looking out the window at my brothers and sister and the other neighborhood children playing outside. I had begun coughing and wheezing again, so I would have to go back to my asthma tent.

Hearing me coughing, my mother came into the room to refill the vaporizer with Vicks. "All right, Tommie," she said, "it's time to get back under the tent."

"But, Momma," I protested, "I'm tired of that old tent every year. I miss half of my summer having to stay under that crazy tent. Why can't I play like the other kids?"

"Well, son," she answered, "you take this Bible and read it, and God will heal you. Remember, tomorrow you have a doctor's visit."

The next day, at the inner-city clinic where we got treated, a Black doctor gave me a shot. Oh, I hated that! A few hours later, I was having a bad reaction. As it turned out, the doctor had given me the wrong shot. My eyes were big and dilated, and I was sweating and gasping for breath. Mom and my brothers and sister were frantic.

"Little T. is dying!" someone said. They told me to hold on, that Dad was racing home to take me to the hospital.

Dad arrived, and my oldest brother burst into the room and grabbed me up from the bed. I was holding on to the Bible my Momma had given me. I had been reading it, like she told me to.

"Come on," my big brother said, "Daddy is here! Let's go! Let's go!" He put me on his shoulders and ran for the car. As they raced me to the hospital, I never let go of that Bible.

Dad was furious. "Betty," he said, "the longest day you live, don't you ever take my child to a @%$^*& *&^%$# Black doctor.

Unfortunately, in junior high, as I will tell later, I got away from God. By the time I was in my early twenties, I was married, had formed my own R&B band, and was playing the clubs.

One day I had parked the big painted school bus the band used to get from gig to gig in front of Mom's house. I and the other band members were bringing out and loading the last pieces of music equipment for an out-of-town gig in Shreveport, Louisiana. While I was still inside, my old-fashioned Pentecostal mother peeked her head out the door and then walked over to the front of the bus in a sly manner, laid her hands on the hood, and began praying quietly in tongues.

When I came walking up with my muscle shirt and jeans on, I stopped to talk with her, as the others got on the bus and waited.

"Hi Mom," I said, "we're headed out of town. And, Mom, I know what you're doing. That holly rollie stuff."

Mom just smiled. Then, suddenly, she got serious. "Son, take the Lord with you wherever you go!"

Then, seemingly as an afterthought, she added, "And you know one day you're going to preach."

"Come on now, Momma," I protested. "We've got enough preachers in the family already."

"Yes," she answered, "but not many chosen. The Bible says, 'Many are called, but few are chosen.' "

Hurrying, trying not to get into a religious thing with my mom, I waved at her and said in a loving manner, "Okay, Mom. We're running behind, so we've got to roll."

Later that evening, at twilight, the bus was speeding down the road. I had been smoking marijuana and was driving with a bottle of cheap cold wine in one hand and my favorite hat turned backward. The wind and rain blew off one of our windshield wipers, so Ricky, our guitar player, had to lean out the passenger side of the bus and keep wiping the window with a towel. As usual, the converted school bus, with two huge pictures of the group painted on it sides, was drawing a lot of attention.

The other members of the band were buzzing from the marijuana. We had also brought my wife, another band member's wife, and some girlfriends, and they were all laughing and having a good time in the back. One of the band members we called Fat Man called out to me, "Hey T, you need to slow this bus down, dude. Negro, you gonna kill us all." We were going too fast on a narrow road.

My brother Richard, a singer with the band, chimed in, "Yeah, T, let Ricky drive."

But I wasn't about to give up my spot. "Hey, Negroes," I said, "I'm driving this bus. You punks just need to chill." They quieted down, but then, suddenly the bus veered out of control and slid into a deep ditch on the side of the road. The ditch was so deep that the bus was tilted, leaning sideways. Frantic, everyone onboard screamed and cursed at me, blaming me for my carelessness.

Fat said, "See, Negro, I told you!"

Richard shouted, "Hey, you guys, chill!" Then he added, "Don't nobody move. You could tilt the bus into the ditch."

"Yea, man, you all cool it!" Rich added, and the two of them slowly walked over to look through the bus window, assessing the danger. They were disturbed to see just how deep the ditch was.

Ricky drew back in fear, "Don't anybody move!" he warned. Turning to me, he said, "This isn't good, man!"

At first, I was looking around the bus, trying to think what we should do, but then I slowly put my head down on the steering wheel. Everybody was quiet, but I had seen the fear in their eyes.

Richard was calm. "Everybody move to the other side of bus to balance it," he suggested.

My head was still down, and I was remembering my mother laying hands on the bus and praying. Now, I, too, prayed quietly. "God, I don't know You like my mother does, but we need Your help right now. Help us, Lord, and I will write songs for You and will help Your people. My mother's prayers apparently kept us from going all the way over, so will You hear my prayers to bring us out of here?" Then I raised my head and looked around at everyone.

By now, onlookers had gathered, and they were warning us all not to move or the bus would flip on over. Suddenly emboldened, I spoke up, "Be still, everyone! We're coming out of here!" Then I cranked the bus up. When I did that, suddenly a wind came out of nowhere and engulfed the whole vehicle. As I tried to move it, you could hear gears shifting, the motor roaring, and something seemed to be pushing the bus back onto the road.

The members of the band shouted out, "All right! Cool!" There was clapping and laughing inside the bus and also from the onlookers outside.

Later that night, inside a Louisiana nightclub, the band was on stage, playing to a packed crowd and waiting for Stan the Man, our announcer, to come up and introduce the singing group. But back in the dressing room, the other members of the group were arguing with me. I had said, "Hey, man, God kept us tonight, so we should have a prayer before we go out," but that didn't go over well.

"Dude," one of the singers objected, "we're not here to pray. Man, I feeling my high and you trying to blow it!"

Poochey, another member, was in a corner drinking beer and smoking a cigarette. "Man, T," he said, "You need to chill on that prayer stuff."

"Hey," I insisted, "I'm the darn group manager and you jokers blew it with the Judge and Phillie Records, not wanting Mama Lou to sing with us. I'm not going to take no vote on this. We are gonna pray, and that's it. ... Or I'm not going out."

Fat Man and Poochey kept arguing with me, and then they got in each other's face, and the rest of the group had to break it up.

Fat Man tried cracking a joke: "This brother need to be singing with the blind boys or some church choir or something."

Just then there was a knock at the door, and I cracked it open. Standing there were five women, trying to push their way in to meet the singers. I forced the door shut and locked it. "This is not the time for no women," I said. "It's time to pray." I was determined that I was not going out there unless we honored God in prayer first.

The announcer had already started announcing the group some five minutes earlier, and he was now stalling for time by telling jokes. He was wondering what was going on.

Richard wanted to settle the tension, so he said, "Look, brothers, let's just go on and pray. We gotta get paid cause I got my woman with me!"

Anthony chimed in, "Hey man, let's go on and do this."

They all gathered around me and I said a prayer. As the group finally ran toward the stage, the crowd cheered.

When we came to our last song that night, I took the mic and said, "We want to dedicate this next song to our God for sparing our lives earlier today on the highway." Then we sang *I Believe* by the Ebony's, and the crowd gave us a standing ovation. Richard and I led the song, and that night I felt something I had never felt before. In my heart, I knew that I would be leaving the group and the club scene before very long. Three years later, I did just that.

CHAPTER 6

THE CALLING AND THE COMMISSIONING

There was a time when my sister, who was then in her late thirties, would be out in the clubs hanging out with the party crowd. Despite repeated warnings from my mother about the danger of being with married men, she hadn't taken heed. I can never forget what happened one Friday night.

I had stopped by my parents' house and, as I was coming out of Mom's kitchen (eating a piece of chicken I had stolen from the pot), I could hear my sister banging at the door. My nephew answered the door before I could get to it, and my sister came in screaming at the top of her lungs.

Mom came running out of her bedroom, trying to calm my sister down. But then my sister started rolling on the floor like an animal and grabbing and pulling her hair like a crazy person. Mom seemed to be just looking at her, but then she said, "I know what's wrong with her!" She hurried to the phone and called her spiritual mother, an old Pentecostal prayer warrior we called Momma Bonna. I was looking at all of this in awe.

After talking with Momma Bonna for a few minutes, Mom calmly put the phone down, went to the kitchen and

49

got a glass of water. She got back on the phone and began to pray with her prayer partner. In the meantime, my sister was tearing up the front room and screaming at the top of her lungs. My eyes were as big as fifty cent pieces, as I watched this all unfolding.

When Mom put down the phone, she boldly walked over to my sister and stood before her. She had stopped praying now. She held the glass of water straight out and said, "In the name of Jesus!" And then she breathed on it and poured the water over my sister's head. My sister's eyes began to roll to the back of her head, and she suddenly calmed down and then seemed to faint.

Mom stood over my sister, and within a few minutes, she slowly got up and was looking around the room. She was totally healed. She sat down in a chair, as if she was just waking up from a trance or a deep sleep. Mom bent over her and told her, "The married man you were with to-night ... his wife has put a spell on you. Stay away from sin and, even more so, stay away from married men."

My sister shook her head in agreement, said, "Okay," put her wig back on, and went back to her car where her girlfriends were waiting, and they drove off. This whole episode blew me away, and I found myself standing there frozen with the chicken still in my hand.

When I was twenty-one, one day I was again visiting my parents' house, this time waiting for my dad to come home from work. I was suffering from a bad headache and was hung over from being out all night the night before. I experienced these headaches frequently while working the nightclub scene around Houston, some-times performing all night long as a singer and guitarist with the band.

A woman we called Mother Mike was there that day. Mother Mike was Mom's closet friend, she was a strong and powerful Pentecostal minister, and she was like a second mother to us children. When we were still small, we had called her Big Mike because of her size. She saw me holding my head and started walking toward me.

I thought to myself, *Oh, Lord, here she comes to preach to me!* But this time Momma Mike didn't preach. Instead, she said, "Boy, you are running from God and His calling," and she laid her hands on my forehead. When she did this, the headache disappeared instantly.

This was the icing on the cake. For years I had been prayed for by my mother, who was also a Church of God in Christ (COGIC) Missionary Minister. As children, we had called her the Big Moose. Until junior high, my parents had been very proud of me for being an honor student. I have to give a lot of credit to my teachers. After seeing my IQ test scores, they understood that I was bored with the regular class curriculum, and they joined together to give me extra after-school activities.

These teachers knew how to push me. They were determined to see me go to MIT (Massachusetts Institute of Technology) one day. And I was doing very well ... until I got in with the wrong crowd, a very fast crowd of guys, and my life took a downward spiral.

Now I began coming home high on drugs. Mom would be speaking in tongues and saying, "Yes, Lord," and go right to the drugs I had hidden in the house. But, when she tried to lay hands on me, I would shout out, "Don't do that!" Many times I ran from the house and even jumped through a window, trying to get away from her, but she would be right behind me, praying, "Lord, touch him! Use him to preach Your Word!"

My guys and I continued to get high and then would go to a different friend's house each day to chill out in their bedroom. But all of my buddies were afraid to come to our house because they were afraid of my mother, thinking that she was using some kind of witchcraft (or something) because whenever she touched any of us, something would go all over us. I now know what that "something" was. It was the Holy Ghost. I saw many miracles that God worked through my mother that I don't have space to tell here.

After Mother Mike touched me and brought me healing, two years later, at the age of twenty-three, I found myself a junior deacon at Outreach Missionary Baptist Church, and I was searching for more. I still felt empty and didn't see the power or the presence I was used to seeing in my mother and in Mother Mike. It wasn't until two years later, when I was twenty-five, that I was gloriously saved, filled with the baptism of the Holy Ghost and called into the ministry.

That baptism was so miraculous. It happened after I had been reading a book by Oral Roberts entitled *You Can Be Filled with the Spirit.* I had also been sneaking out to a Holiness Revival Center Church revival in Houston, where the pastor was a powerful apostle in the Kingdom and operated in the prophetic and miracle ministries.

It all happened in my bedroom one evening after I had come home from work. There, in that humble bedroom, I traveled through the skies and was taken up into the heavens. I landed in a room where I saw the apostles gathered around a dinner table. At the head of the table was a big glow, and to the right of that glow was Jesus. He had been looking at me since I landed, and now they all turned and looked at me. It was an amazing experience!

The lights were warm, and the colors were so beautiful. The atmosphere was amazing. I said, "Lord, it is good to be here." I was standing on the opposite end of the table, about twenty feet away from Him.

He said, "I know, but you must go back."

As I opened my mouth to ask if I could stay, Jesus lifted one of His hands in the air, swung it at me and blew, pushing the air my way like a wind. This wind hit me with so much force that it knocked me up into the air and back out into the clouds in space.

I remember saying, "OOOOOH, WOW!" as my body fell backward, twirling through time and space. After a few minutes I landed back in my body in the bedroom, and I was speaking in tongues. Jesus had blown on me for the anointing and the Holy Ghost.

Then, as I was kneeling there, Jesus came walking into my bedroom. His glow lit up my room. He walked up to me, stood over me smiling, and said, "Go ahead and preach My Word. Pray for the sick and the afflicted. Be not afraid of anything or anyone, for thou shall be a prophet unto this generation. Thy shalt do all things through Me, for I will strengthen you."

After that, He turned and walked away, up into the clouds and back into Heaven. The atmosphere was so colorful, so warm, so beautiful, so serene and so calm. I heard heavenly music, and it was all indescribably beautiful.

The glory left in my room made me so happy I started smiling, laughing out loud and rolling on the floor like a drunken man. I tried to walk and couldn't. I just lay on the floor, laughing so loud my wife came in and just looked at me. She was shocked and said to me, "Man, what are you drinking? Or have you been using drugs again?" I tried to get up off the floor and talk to her, but I could only speak gibberish like a drunkard. I had done all kinds of drugs in my day, but this was the best I had ever felt.

Just as soon as I was able, I made my way to the telephone in the kitchen and called my mother. When she answered, all I could do was burst out in clear-flowing tongues. She said, "Tommie, is this you?"

I said, "Yeah, Momma, it's me."

She said, "Let me call you right back. When the phone rang, she had with her, on the line, all of her sisters who were COGIC church missionaries in Fort Worth. They asked me what had happened, but when I tried to tell them, my words came out in tongues.

I heard my auntie and another old church mother say, "Betty, your son got the real thing. It's the Holy Ghost." They all shouted, and we spoke in tongues together for an hour or more, even prophesying.

I preached my first sermon at the Baptist church I had been attending. I had been a junior deacon there for two years by then, but, as I shared earlier, had been sneaking off at times to the Holiness Revival Church. My whole family was there to hear my first sermon: my wife, mother, father, Mother Mike and my brothers, along with a new mother in the Lord I had met while visiting around (I will call her Mother C). She was also a COGIC evangelist and missionary (which is what the COGIC called their women ministers and church elders).

The church was full that day, and I was excited but nervous to take the platform. As I was praying back in the minister's quarters, I began to pray in tongues, and all the other young ministers looked at me weird when I came out. My oldest brother overheard a visiting pastor tell my pastor, "You've got problems now. They say he speaks in tongues, doctor. Believe me, you are going to have problems with him." I didn't know this until afterward, but I did feel the tension between my mother's Pentecostal guests and the pastor.

After being finally called up, I made small talk for a few minutes and then went right into my sermon, pulling out my notes. My message title was "This Same Jesus," and it was taken from a story in Acts 1:11:

Which also said, Ye men of Galilee, why stand ye gazing up into heaven? THIS SAME JESUS, which is taken up from you into heaven shall so come in like manner as ye have seen him go into heaven.

The message did not come easily. I was wrestling with this new-found pressure that was trying to hinder me, and after about ten minutes of trying to get a flow going, the wind blew one of my teaching sheets over, as if it were turning a page in a book. Suddenly, something hit me, and I felt the power of God come all over me. I grabbed the rest of my notes, threw them on the floor and began to preach under the anointing, even prophesying.

The people who were present, especially Mom's group, began to get with me, as the Spirit moved throughout the congregation. Some people were slain in the Spirit, and others began shouting and running. God had showed up.

I remember looking back at my pastor at one point. He tried to hide it, but he had a worried look on his face, as if his church was falling into chaos. In order not to offend him, I stopped what I was doing and made an altar call for souls. That always goes over well in a Baptist church.

I really appreciated my pastor, and not just as a pastor, but also as a friend. The two of us hung out together a lot.

After the altar call for salvation, I made a call for healing, not looking at the pastor now, but trying to obey God. Some came up for healing. I will never forget a lady and her boyfriend who came for prayer. The lady was battling a shoulder condition, and when I began to pray for her the demons in her started manifesting. I saw Missionary C, my friend and mentor, who was a COGIC missionary evangelist, go toward her.

Immediately I said, "Missionary C, don't touch her. Just stretch your hands out toward her." But Missionary C didn't listen. She went to the lady and laid hands on her. As soon as the COGIC missionary laid hands on the woman, she jumped back and said, "Ouch," and grabbed her shoulder. I went down from the platform and began binding the demons in the sick lady, and she fell out, slain in the Spirit.

It was then that I witnessed something I had never seen before. The evil spirit jumped out of her, looked at me and tried to bluff me. I shouted, "Get out of here." Slowly and stubbornly he looked around and then started walking down the aisle toward the back door.

That demon was horrible looking, with an opaque misty face, red eyes and a black neck. Half of his body was tar black, and the other half was opaque white. As I walked down the isle, telling the spirit to go, most of the Baptist members looked at me as if I had lost my mind. Being a novice at ministry, I wondered why they weren't seeing what I was seeing.

When the demon made it to the back door, he turned and looked at me and tried to frighten me again by pointing at me and saying, "I am gonna get you!"

I shouted out for the final time and said, "Out of here, in Jesus' name." He whimpered, and then turned and ran out of the building.

I will never forget that day. After my sermon, my dad stood and expressed how proud he was of me. That was truly a blessing to me after I had given him and my mother more trials and disappointments than all my other brothers and sister combined. He was a construction worker who had worked hard all his life to raise us, while my mother worked in wealthy homes and hotels as a maid. Now they were witnessing their son being empowered to do the things of God.

CHAPTER 7

THE GIFT OF PROPHECY

The years I spent from the age of twenty-five through fifty-five were very exciting ones of miracle prophetic growth, but also of prophetic pain. I had to learn many things about life and about God during that time. I feel it is appropriate to highlight special ministry events and times in my life in this chapter.

As I mentioned in the previous chapter, I had a pastor from whom I learned many things. One of those things was God's order. I was about to learn another lesson. God had destined me to have a prophetic gift.

MY VISION OF HURRICANES KATRINA AND RITA, SPOKEN TO A LOCAL ASSEMBLY WHILE IN A REVIVAL

About a month after my first sermon I had a vision in which I foresaw Hurricane Rita. According to Wikipedia, "Hurricane Rita (September 21, 2005) was the fourth-most intense Atlantic hurricane ever recorded and the most intense tropical cyclone ever observed in the Gulf of Mexico. It was part of the record-breaking 2005 Atlantic Hurricane Season, which included three of the six most intense Atlantic hurricanes ever recorded. ... Rita was the eighteenth named storm, tenth hurricane, and fifth major hurricane of the 2005 season. ... Electric service was disrupted in some areas of both Texas and Louisiana for several weeks. Texas reported the most deaths from the hurricane, where 113 deaths were reported, 107 of which were associated with the evacuation of the Houston metropolitan area." [1]

It was August of 2005, a calm night in Eagle Lake, a little Texas country town about sixty-seven miles below Houston.

1. https://en.wikipedia.org/wiki/Hurricane_Rita

I was up on the platform preaching a revival service for Pastor David Jones, a very dear friend, when, suddenly, in the middle of my message, I stopped preaching and said, "There's a hurricane coming. There's a hurricane coming toward Houston. Do not leave, but go to the church. Stay in the church, do not leave." Then I immediately went back to my sermon for that night.

Some forty-five days later Hurricane Rita was spotted heading toward Houston. There was mass pandemonium and chaos in the streets and highways in and around the city and the surrounding counties, with everyone thinking Houston would receive the same devastation as New Orleans had from Hurricane Katrina.

With a mass exodus taking place, the pastor's precious wife and others of the church asked him what he thought they should do. He reminded them all of what I had said, "Do not leave; stay in the church." He and his wife came into agreement and elected to go to the church and ride out the hurricane there, along with their members.

One lady member, a beautiful young woman, called the pastor, insisting that she was determined to get out ahead of the storm. The pastor begged her not to get on the road but, rather, to obey the prophetic word from God's servant. She didn't listen, and later called back, frantic, begging for someone to come and get her. She was stuck on the road in the middle of that chaos. The majority of the congregation obeyed the prophecy and had church that night and had a great time of fellowship, while other people were stranded, out of gas, and getting sick and even dying on the roadways. God knows what is best and uses His prophets to advise us.

God's Word teaches us about prophets and prophecy:

Surely the LORD GOD does nothing; unless He reveals his secret to his servants the prophets.
                                        Amos 3:7

Listening to God's prophets is for our benefit. It's in the Bible:

Hear me, O Judah, and ye inhabitants of Jerusalem; Believe in the LORD your GOD, so shall ye be established; believe his prophets, so shall ye prosper.
                                        2 Chronicles 20:20

What are some ways God communicated to His prophets? It's in the Bible:

Hear now my words: If there is a prophet among you, I, the LORD, make myself known unto him in a vision; I speak to him in a dream.
                                        Numbers 12:6

God uses prophets to guide His people into the perfect will and direction of the Lord. It's in the Bible:

Yet he sent prophets to them, to bring them again unto the LORD; and they testified against them: but they would not give ear. 2 Chronicles 24:19

Here are some things that I prophesied under the Spirit in those days, which all came to pass:

- The fall and subsequent rise again of Minister Jim Baker of PTL
- The fall of Jimmy Swaggart of Jimmy Swaggart Ministries and his rebirth as a major television and satellite network
- The finding of a runaway daughter (found at her cousin's home in Louisiana)
- The shutting down of the witches in Houston
- The election of President Ronald Reagan a year in advance of it happening
- The election of President Donald J. Trump a year in advance of it happening
- A two-month prior warning of Hurricane Alicia in 1983
- A two-month warning of the coming of Hurricane Rita and an admonishment to the church members to stay in the church building when it did come
- A movie produced exposing Planned Parenthood and their selling of baby parts

Here are some things I prophesied that are yet to come:

- I saw Heaven as a very fun place
- I saw army tanks on the city streets of America with curfews in place while Donald Trump is President
- I saw calamity in our streets and a resulting revival taking place in America
- I saw a great revival sweeping Israel, as the news out of Israel shocks the whole world

THE PROPHECY OF JIM BAKER AND THE PTL FALL AND REBIRTH

One day, as I was watching the PTL Show with Jim and Tammy Baker on TV, God spoke to me and said, "Everything you see there will come to an end." I called the man who was my pastor at the time and shared this with him. He was sympathetic and gentle with me, realizing that I was a baby Christian, but, at the same time, he tried hard to explain it all away.

Then God told me to write to the Bakers to share this warning with them. Out of respect for my pastor, I never did. Of course, it was too late when the ministry then fell.

In a vision I had about Jim Baker, there was a twenty-foot-long two-legged beast that wore Medieval or Roman war clothing. With helmet and all, he stood atop a tall mountain. Down below, Christians were mounting up, but they had to go up that mountain to get to Heaven. It seemed as though the beast was their final challenge, the final effort to stop them from victory and keep them from going to Heaven.

Believers began making their way up the mountain, with their hands in the air, praising God, and Jim Baker was leading them. As they got closer and closer, their praises began to bind the beast and cause him much discomfort.

The beast responded by shooting powerful arrows down at them. You could feel the intense heat and hear the incredible hissing and swishing sound the arrows made, as they flew by, missing the Christians. Sadly, however, as the believers got closer and closer, the intense flurry of arrows began to hit some of them with a loud thumping sound. It was unforgettable.

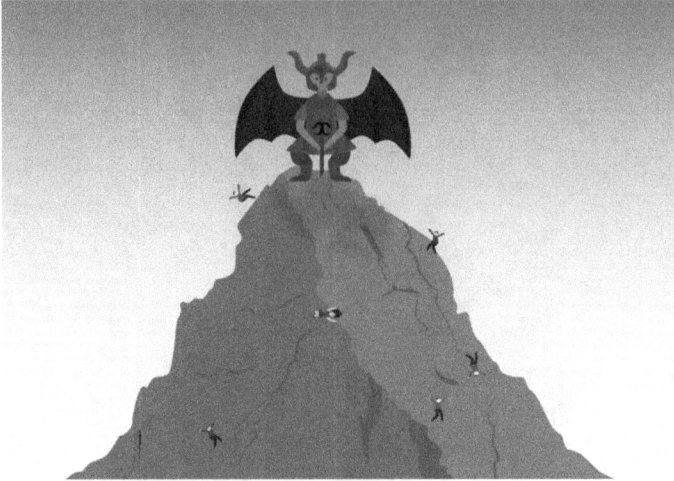

As an arrow would hit a believer, it would lift them into the air and drop them more than a hundred feet backward to the ground below. Some arrows were so powerful that they had ten or more believers on them, all hit by the same arrow.

Jim Baker ordered the healthy believers to go and help the wounded ones. One would get on their left and another on their right, and they wrapped their wounded arms around their own neck with one hand, while continuing to praise God with the other. Then two believers would get behind the wounded and push with one hand, while continuing to praise with the other, and two would get in front of the wounded person and pull them with one hand, while praising God with the other. This love and unity became so powerful that God's people could not be stopped, and ultimately they toppled the big giant, causing him to fall over a cliff.

It was two years later when all the scandal hit the airwaves, leading to the crash of PTL. I was very hurt by this because a year earlier I'd had a powerful dream in which I visited PTL and met Jim Baker. We were together in the prayer room and I asked him how to build a PTL in Houston.

In the dream, he stood in front of me, planted his feet apart, and bent over in a football player's blocking position. Then he said, "To build something like this, you've got to plant your feet and have the tenacity of a bulldog. You can't be moved by anyone or anything."

Ironically, years later, after I'd had the vision, I was a guest on a TV show and told the television audience (I still have the videotape) that I foresaw Jim Baker being released from prison and then continuing the vision of taking God's people to the mountaintop and, in fact, going on to build a more powerful television ministry than before.

In May of 2017 the Lord revealed to me that millions of people will be lost and give up who did not listen to Jim Baker's warnings to prepare. The Lord said He has several ministers whom He has ordained and commissioned to take His believers through the last Red Sea End-Time experience to the Promised Land, and Jim Baker is one of them.

DEMONIC DELIVERANCE AT THE REAL ROCK

One Friday night in the early 1980s, I was preaching at the Real Rock Church and Drug Reform Home. The home was located on the church property, but it sat on its own acreage. It was frequented by all the local major news networks, such as Fox 26 News and ABC 13, because it was being touted as the first cutting-edge, church-run facility actually helping thousands of adults and young people to get set free from drugs and alcohol addiction. These restorations were the present buzz in the city, and TV networks sent crews to film most graduations.

Looking back, the news interviews we did in those days helped us to meet millionaires, some of whom became serious financial sponsors, and also to meet prominent city officials. The interviews also lead to a beautiful merger of our efforts with those of the Houston Police Department, and in this way we were able to lower crime in the South Acres area of South Park significantly.

That night I was up ministering and praying for men and women who had come to the home for help. The service was nearing an end when one of the female residents in the program came up for prayer. As I prayed for her, it didn't take long to realize that she was demon possessed. Her body actually started to swell and contort.

Because I had built my ministry around deliverance years earlier these types of manifestations were nothing new to me. I was well supported by pastors, leaders and families who would call on me for what many know as an "exorcism," but my team always called it "a demonic deliverance."

The young lady started to scream as we called the demons out of her. She was so strong that she grabbed one of the minsters next to me, Minister Boyd, and threw him across the room. For a few moments, things got very violent, as we tried to get control of her raging and jerking body movements.

I kept casting out the devils in Jesus' name, and she finally fell to the floor whimpering. As other minsters held her down, I knelt over her, screaming out, "What's your name?"

Minister Johnnie Winters, my nephew, who had assisted me in many deliverances, screamed out, "Pastor! Pastor, her body is swelling!"

I immediately screamed out, "What's your name? What's your name?"

I got eye to eye with her, and she cried out, "My name is suicide. Suicide!" Then she roared like a lion.

After casting out the suicide demon, I yelled out again, "What's your name?"

She screamed out, "Crack!"

After minutes of our casting that spirit and others out, she finally whispered her name and fainted (we call it being slain in the Spirit), and I went back to speaking to the church.

Ten minutes later the woman woke up, and we lifted her from the floor. She appeared to be okay. I pointed to Heaven as the church gave a round of applause, thinking that she was completely free.

Usually, after any service is over, someone from my team follows up with those who have gone through deliverance, but this time, for some reason, no one did. Being very hungry, we quickly headed out to our favorite late-night dinner spot, to talk and fellowship. We were eating there and having great fellowship when suddenly an emergency page came through. (Back in those days before cell phones, pagers were our main communications device.)

I immediately gave the information to my right-hand man, Epstein D. Henry, the drug reform home's grounds manager, to call the church back. Epstein himself had come to our program as a crack addict and ex-con who, because of drugs, had missed opportunities for a promising basketball career, playing with the likes of Clyde Drexler. (Epstein was six feet five inches tall.)

After Epstein called the church, we were told we needed to come back there immediately. He told me, "It looks like the demons came back on the lady we prayed for."

As we pulled up onto the church property, we all got out and ran to the ladies' dormitory. Everyone was standing outside, both the women who lived there and the forty men who were also in the drug reform program. As we made our way to the dorm, it was through a crowd of frightened men and recovering residents. They all acted as if they had seen a ghost.

Running up to the entrance and then walking in, I was somewhat surprised at what I saw next. The lady was in a corner growling at the men who stood a safe and fearful distance of at least ten feet from her. As she would move forward, they would move back.

I was so proud and thrilled to see my oldest son, Terzeno, at the front of the line, leading the charge. I watched him and the residents imitate me and the team. They kept saying, "What's your name? What's your name?" There was nothing funny about what was happening, but I have to be honest and say that I found the whole thing rather humorous.

I watched the efforts of the others for a few minutes, but when they realized I was there, they had no problems turning things over to me and the team. I have to give them a C for trying.

After taking charge, it wasn't long before we were able to get the remaining demons out of the woman. We instructed the young lady to attend our healing classes to keep her under the Word of God. Today she is a minister in a local church. Ironically, she is the daughter of prominent pastors.

That night, we lost several grown male residents who were frightened out of their minds, never having experienced anything quite like that. It was the talk of the program and also of people in the community for many years to come. God had called me to a ministry of the prophetic and the miraculous, of deliverance for the captives.

Part III

Just Before the Last Seven Days

CHAPTER 8

WHAT I SAW

WHAT I SAW RELATED TO THE CHURCH

Part of the reason I have shared a portion of my testimony here is so that you will know where I am coming from as I relate to you my visions of the end time.

In one vision, a train took us to some of the churches which had become entertainment centers, with game rooms and even a sports bar, with restaurants—the whole works. The church leaders were no longer referred to as pastors, but as directors, and there was no preaching for salvation but only fifteen minutes of very light teaching. The message was totally about grace and love, and it was frowned upon to preach about the cross or sin or Hell.

Other churches, filled to capacity, were operating like emergency shelters for those who were sick, suffering and lacking the strength to fight any longer. Suddenly I and a few other ministers stood up and rallied the people. People started getting up and encouraging and helping each other. Those in beds started getting up and throwing the sheets from their sick beds on the ground. Miracles were happening.

The next vision showed the people in the church. I was encouraging the church not to give up. I was saying, "Some of you are going to give up, and some of you are going to be sacrificed. But I urge you, Please don't give up. God will see you through it." Many got on the train with us that day.

WHAT I SAW RELATED TO THE GAY COMMUNITY

At a certain park, there were some policeman doing security duty when a gay group came through taunting the young men and women and young girls. The gay men and women began to grope some of the young people. One of the young officers said, "That's enough! I'm going to stop this."

His partner grabbed him and said, "You're going to get us all in hot water, bothering these gays." The young officer wanted to cry, as he realized he was powerless against the gay community.

We looked again, and now the gays had taken over several churches and demanded that the pastors approve of their lifestyle. Some did. Those who approved were later made to perform gay marriages and even to ordain gay ministers and attend gay events. Later, some of those ministers became gay themselves.

I remember seeing a pastor being raped and humiliated by seven gay men at mid-day in a church. He fell over onto the Bible, and the place where it was opened said:

For this cause God gave them up unto vile affections: for even their women did change the natural use into that which is against nature: and likewise also the men, leaving the natural use of the woman, burned in their lust one toward another; men with men working that which is unseemly, and receiving in themselves that recompence of their error which was meet. And even as they did not like to retain God in their knowledge, God gave them over to a reprobate mind, to do those things which are not convenient. ...

Who knowing the judgment of God, that they which commit such things are worthy of death, not only do the same, but have pleasure in them that do them.

Romans 1:26-28 and 32

The gay community even had their own parks in various cities, and those parks were off limits to everyone else. Those gay parks were filled with open sex between young people and grown-ups. These places had become safe havens when men could commit lewd sex acts and kidnappings. But they had developed a new term for it, one that was more politically acceptable, and they demanded to be called by that new term, no longer what they really were.

The gays also had introduced a new course in school that everyone was required to take. As a result, it was more of a crime when a boy touched a girl student than when a boy touched another boy student.

Big businesses were afraid of the gays and had to hire them and even promote their lifestyle. A doctor was on television announcing a new plague that was affecting the gay community across the nation.

There were entire gay community townhouses and community developments and schools. Even though many churches and individuals still held to their standards, most had given in to gay demands and were happy to see the gays with the rest of their population. Needless to say, they did not get on the train.

WHAT I SAW RELATED TO THE TREATMENT OF ANIMALS

I saw that animals were being treated better than human babies. It was as if the animals were almost being worshiped like gods, while many people were being killed. New laws made it a felony for certain offenses against animals. Dogs had become more popular than humans, and you could go to jail for a long time for injuring a dog. The truth is that many of the pets, mostly the dogs, were sex toys. They would never tell, so they were being sexually abused by men.

WHAT I SAW RELATED TO THE POLITICAL SYSTEM

I saw that the political system was no longer the same. A great paradigm shift had come. In an open vision one day I saw the media moguls from all over the world gathered at a large mansion. They had made a pact to use their media to bring world peace. Actually, what they wanted and were focused on was controlling America. There was an agreement among them to puff up or build up controversy with the aim of controlling elections, businesses, politicians and communities.

I saw Fox News coming under attack from our government but also from a foreign nation. It seemed that the other media moguls were in agreement to try to shut down Fox News and bankrupt it. There was also an organized effort to stop Christian television in America, but the movement had started in other nations and been successful there first.

This group was even strategic in causing Christians to fight each other, and this caused chaos within communities. Many Christian broadcasters and religious newscasters started migrating to Fox News and other conservative Christian-based networks. News networks now had even more power and were viewed by many as the new prophets of our time, especially during times of disaster and crises.

And that was just the beginning. I saw much more in visions of *The Last Seven Days* on Earth.

Part IV

The Last Seven Days

CHAPTER 9

DAY 1—THE EVIL SPIRIT

As I sat in a huge facility, or what I call the Elect's Building or the Spot, I began to talk with several of the elect individuals who were sitting near me and to listen to their victory stories. We were all aware that the world was being destroyed, or purged, as we had been taught it would be.

It is totally impossible to describe the glowing beauty and perfectly scented aroma of the beautiful swirling winds that formed a transparent shield around us. That shield kept the fires and heat away from our building, even as the winds kept our building nice and cool through the whole process.

I was awed by the fact that there were only twelve of us. We seemed to be the only ones chosen to see what was happening on Earth. It was as if everyone else had been shielded from seeing this horrible purging event.

The morning started with news networks warning viewers how to try to stay safe from the intense heat that was emanating from an unknown source. They were interviewing climate-change experts, trying to find some answer to the riddle. Since people were continuing with their regular lifestyles of heated gossip, climate change and the emissions from chemical plants were being most commonly blamed for it all. This dominated the day's conversations. In the meantime, the day grew hotter.

There were fans in windows and cars breaking down, as people attempted to go to work and go about their daily business.

HEAT FROM THE HAILSTONES

Some cities were being hit by rain, with unusual milky-looking hailstones that had a strong gas scent about them. At this point of the first day, people were thinking the intense heat would soon dissipate. However, by around 3 P.M. that afternoon it had gotten even hotter, and as people began to feel the heat, tensions began to rise.

Another news report had a city official and other city leaders blaming climate change. That was when things started to happen. At 3 P.M. a breaking news story came on naming city after city and warning everyone in those cities not to go outside because a mysterious strong-smelling gas was coming from the hailstones. People in cities around the nation were warned to hunker down and shelter in place until the crisis blew over.

There was a cut to a news reporter interviewing a scientist who felt that the heat was coming from the hailstones. Then I saw flashes of people beginning to panic and getting agitated as the heat continued to rise. For many, the pungent smell of gas was another cause for panic.

In another flashed scene, people were running to take cover in hotels, stores and other public buildings, and homes were being boarded up. Some families were seen arguing about what they should do.

Around 3:15 P.M. the whole world suddenly stood still, as a massive earthquake shook the whole Earth. The force of it was unbelievable. Everyone felt the shaking, and people were screaming everywhere.

As I looked into a big mirror, I only saw what was happening in America and other nearby countries that our building covered. Because I could see a number of other buildings covered by the winds, but I could not see what they saw. I could get only quick glimpses of the other countries being destroyed.

No roads were now passable, and airplanes were said to be crashing on take-off.

THE FELLOWSHIP INSIDE THE WIND-COVERED BUILDING

Meanwhile, inside the room there were individuals I had met in the purging rooms a few days earlier. They greeted each other and began to fellowship.

Then, an angelic-looking being came up to us and said, "Get it all out now because when the Lord comes the first thing He is going to do is wipe away all your tears and all your sorrows and bad memories." Everyone looked amazed at each other and began to open up.

One man said, "I am E.J. Oday, and I am a Pentecostal evangelist and former drug dealer. This is my wife Gloria, and she does home schooling for our kids." Gloria nodded her head politely, looked over at her kids in the kid's section, and smiled.

E.J. said, "I thank God for His deliverance. Jim, we are so blessed to be here. Just look out there."

Jim said, "The whole world is being purged. We were all amazed as we briefly looked into the movie-like screen that showed what was happening to mankind."

"Hi," a woman said, "I am Isabel Love, and I was a real estate agent. And this is my brother Charles."

Charles also spoke, "Hi, I'm Charles Praxton."

Another woman said, "I am Mei Li Cheng, doctor of psychiatry."

"I am Officer Tommie Pendleton, with your local police department," the next man said.

The next in line said, "And I am Raymond Hernandez, a news photographer."

Next was a woman. She said, "I am Lenora Ortega, a journalist."

"Hi," the next in line said, "I am Jim Kaker, and this is my wife Susie. We were the pastors of Glow City Church."

Looking around at everyone and remembering what an angel had said ("say so"), he continued, "Which one of you wants to go first and share your story?"

They all hesitated.

Then Officer Pendleton spoke up. "Well, it seems that everything I dreamed about last night is happening today." All eyes were focused seriously on him, as he continued. "You see, God showed me, while I was in the purging room, some of these events. He told me that on the very first day of the judgment, these events were going to happen.

"First, though, He took me into one of the purging rooms and told me I needed to be delivered from an evil spirit. I was reminded of the Bible passage that says:

Jesus and his disciples arrived on the other side of Lake Galilee, in the territory of Gerasa. As soon as Jesus got out of the boat, he was met by a man who came out of the burial caves there. This man had an evil spirit in him and lived among the tombs.

Nobody could keep him tied with chains any more Many times his feet and his hands had been tied, but every time he broke the chains and smashed the irons on his feet. He was too strong for anyone to control him. Day and night he wandered among the tombs and through the hills, screaming and cutting himself with stones.

He was some distance away when he saw Jesus; so he ran, fell on his knees before Him, and screamed in a loud voice, "Jesus, Son of the Most High God! What do you want with me? For God's sake, I beg you, don't punish me!" (He said this because Jesus was saying, "Evil spirit, come out of this man!")

So Jesus asked him, "What is your name?"

The man answered, "My name is 'Mob'—there are so many of us!" And he kept begging Jesus not to send the evil spirits out of that region.

There was a large herd of pigs nearby, feeding on a hillside. So the spirits begged Jesus, "Send us to the pigs, and let us go into them." He let them go, and the evil spirits went out of the man and entered the pigs. The whole herd—about two thousand pigs in all—rushed down the side of the cliff into the lake and was drowned.

The men who had been taking care of the pigs ran away and spread the news in the town and among the farms. People went out to see what had happened, and when they came to Jesus, they saw the man who used to have the mob of demons in him. He was sitting there, clothed and in his right mind; and they were all afraid. Those who had seen it told the people what had happened to the man with the demons, and about the pigs. Mark 1:5-16, GNT

"You see," Officer Pendleton continued, "as a child I saw my mother killed by a drug dealer. When my father came home and saw what had happened, I begged him to stay with me. 'Don't go, Daddy. Please don't go. Don't leave me, Daddy,' I pleaded.

"My dad said, 'Son, I have to do this. I am going to find them and kill them all,' and he stormed out the door with his gun in hand. But I never saw Daddy again. They murdered him and burned his body.

"In the years to come, I lived with relative after relative. Some were very abusive to me, but I lived for the day I could become a police officer to revenge my parents' death. And, boy, did I. Wow! I was very hard and mean to anyone associated with using or selling drugs. I mean I did some terrible things to those folks. Many times I was happy that dealers would run or try to escape custody so that I could shoot and kill them.

"One day, for instance, I shot a drug dealer, saying that he had been trying to escape. The truth is that I had unlocked the back door of the cruiser and told him I was making a rest-room stop. He hadn't really tried to get away. This kind of conduct went on for the longest time, even spilling over into my marriage and almost destroying it. I was very cruel to my wife.

"At one point, she was attending a Charismatic church and got actively involved in it. One night, when she was away from home in one of their services, I changed the locks on the door. When she came home and couldn't get in, she had to knock on the door. 'Honey,' she called, 'I can't get the door open. Open up. It's cold out here.'

" 'Go back to that church,' I told her, 'and the pastor you're sleeping with.'

" 'No, Tommie, that's not true,' she insisted. 'The devil is playing with your mind.' But I did this to her many more times. Sometimes she would go to sleep praying outside the door, and at other times she would leave, spend the night with friends and then come back the next day.

"One very cold night she knocked and knocked. As usual, she cried out to get in and, as usual, I said no and accused her of adultery with her pastor. She prayed just outside the door. I remember looking out the window after she had been praying out there for at least an hour.

"It was so intensely cold that night. Temperatures had dipped below freezing. I saw her making her way to the car with her Bible in her hand and watched as she got in. I went to the bedroom, got in bed, put on my headset as usual and went to sleep.

"When I woke up the next morning, got ready and left for work, I noticed that her car was still there. I went over to it, not realizing how drastically my life was about to change. As I got closer to my wife's car, I saw her body slumped over with the Bible in her hand. The engine was running, but my wife was dead.

"Now I remembered how she had knocked on the door that night. She had been trying to tell me something, something about her car going off the road and damaging something. Well, that 'something' turned out to be her tailpipe. She had fallen asleep and died from asphyxiation from leaking carbon monoxide fumes.

"I was so filled with remorse that I couldn't bear to touch her. I called my fellow officers, and they sent someone to help me. While they were removing my wife's body from the car, a love letter to me and a petition to the Lord fell from her hand."

Now Officer Pendleton wept as he remembered his wife's final words: "Father, forgive him, for he knows not what he is doing. Make him one of Yours. Save him and fill him with Your precious Holy Spirit. May my love bring him to You."

After a while, Officer Pendleton regained his composure and was able to finish his testimony. "You see, the Bible says *'jealousy is as cruel as the grave.'* Jealousy, envy, revenge and anger are all connected to cause you to hurt and destroy other people. Those are the attributes of an evil spirit, and that's what an evil spirit will cause you to do. Look how it caused the man in the Bible story to cut himself and try to hurt others and it even caused the swine to kill themselves. I gave my life to the Lord two years later and received the gift and have been on God's purging path for several years now."

Then E.J. said, "Officer Pendleton, have you seen your wife since you've been here or spoken with her?"

"Well, people," Officer Pendleton answered, "yes, I saw her today when we arrived. I was only able to wave to her, and she waved back. We smiled at each other and teared up with joy. The Lord said that because of the past circumstances I could not talk to her, but she needed to know her death was not in vain before all of our tears and bad memories are wiped away. As for the Earth, before this first day is over, this is what is about to happen. We will see ..."

My vision suddenly faded to the Earth. People were hurting and frantic, but I could hear Officer Pendleton's voice talking over the scene, narrating what was about to unfold.

Then, suddenly, there was a breaking news report on TV: "Earthquakes are breaking out all over the nation, and no one seems to know what has caused them. NASA scientists are saying that something is going on with the sun. It appears to be moving."

One NASA scientist said, "Well, at this point we are waiting for our computers to supply us the necessary data before we take any measures or come to any conclusions. However, I will say this: people should not worry because this is a once-in-a-lifetime event, and we all know the sun can't move. So, be calm. We, at NASA ... we can fix anything."

But as the day continued, it got hotter and hotter. One breaking report featured an air-conditioning specialist, trying to suggest ways to handle the crisis. He had to admit that air-conditioning units can only drop the air to a certain point, usually fifty percent of the temperature of the air outside. I saw people sweating and hot, using fans in their windows.

The sky was goldish black, and air-conditioning units in homes and cars were breaking down. Then a breaking news report came: medical and scientific authorities were asking that only slender people be allowed to go outside to run errands. They said that larger and heavier people were dying from the heat faster. A man named Doctor Herrington spoke. "Yes," he said, "the body of a smaller-framed and/or tall person has more skin mass to dispel heat than those who are overweight."

Another phenomenon was reported. Dark-skinned people around the world were faring better than their fair-skinned counterparts. It seems that because of the melanin in their skin, they were able to take the heat better. As a result, many African-American people were going from house to house, helping the lighter-skinned races with food and other necessities. On this day, they were heroes for sure, and they were received with open arms, as they met the needs of those who were crying out for help and those needing emergency and special care.

Then the scene shifted back to Officer Pendleton inside the Elect Protective Spot. He was sad, with head bowed, as he made a final statement: "According to my dream, all the people who are evil will die today."

And it was true. All the people who had evil spirits were dying and being burned by the angelic-looking beings that came up out of the ground, out of nowhere, and latched on to certain individuals and burned them to a sizzle.

While this was all happening, the elect looked into the monitors and shook their heads in amazement.

Remember now thy Creator in the days of thy youth, while the evil days come not, nor the years draw nigh, when thou shalt say, I have no pleasure in them; while the sun, or the light, or the moon, or the stars, be not darkened, nor the clouds return after the rain: in the day when the keepers of the house shall tremble, and the strong men shall bow themselves, and the grinders cease because they are few, and those that look out of the windows be darkened, and the doors shall be shut in the streets, when the sound of the grinding is low, and he shall rise up at the voice of the bird, and all the daughters of musick shall be brought low; also when they shall be afraid of that which is high, and fears shall be in the way, and the almond tree shall flourish, and the grasshopper shall be a burden, and desire shall fail: because man goeth to his long home, and the mourners go about the streets. Ecclesiastes 12:1-5

CHAPTER 10

DAY 2 – THE DIVINATION SPIRIT

The elect awakened the next morning and were talking among themselves. Mr. Oday said, "I had a dream."

Isabel Love said, "Well, come on with it, Big Daddy."

All eyes were on E.J., as he spoke with sadness, "In my dream last night, I saw today's events."

"Wow!" Keith said, "it looks like there is a pattern here." They all nodded in agreement.

E.J. continued, "Well, you see, there were seven purging rooms with each room dealing with a particular demonic spirit, right? And each one of us was delivered from a particular demonic attack, right?" He looked around for confirmation.

Isabel Love said, "You are so right. If you recall, in the Bible, Jesus dealt with all seven of the demon spirits and called them by name. I believe that's why He was so successful with demons.

"Today, it's getting hotter by at least ten degrees, and in ten minutes it will be noon. There will be more hailstorms in some places, and afterward it will get even hotter. After today, there will be no more rain."

Doctor Cheng spoke up and said, "You know, hailstorms caused billions of dollars worth of damage in 2016. In north Texas alone, they saw over $1.5 billion in damage."

E.J. said, "In my dream, divination or witchcraft will be destroyed from the Earth," and he then did the voice-over as I saw the events unfolding. People were coming out of their houses, trying to find relief from the heat. At this point, window units and even central air-conditioning units were breaking down and no longer working. Phone lines fell silent, and cell-phone towers began failing. Military jets and other airplanes were crashing because they had nowhere to land. Passenger jets that were circling at the airports eventually ran out of fuel and crashed. People were screaming everywhere. Pandemonium had set in.

Then, television sets suddenly went blank, and there were no more news reports. Television was no longer functioning.

Now I saw the whole Earth suffering from the smothering heat and all those involved in witchcraft were being attacked by angelic-looking demons coming up out of the ground, latching on to them and then exploding into a fiery human-sized fireballs, literally burning that person to ashes with the sizzling sound of bacon being fried:

And it was commanded them that they should not hurt the grass of the earth, neither any green thing, neither any tree; but only those men which have not the seal of God in their foreheads. Revelation 9:4

The heat got worse until people were running around outside naked trying to get relief.

Witch doctors and palm and card readers were chanting, reading and praying to Satan for relief. More than half of Hollywood was being burned up by those underground fire-sizzling-beings. Many actors, band members, the members of singing groups and families that lived by witchcraft were burning and sizzling. The smoke and stench of it was unbearable.

Everybody was horrified, screaming and repenting, but it was too late. The whole world was suffering and powerless, and I saw families in houses, apartments, tents and hospitals showing extreme fear and hopelessness.

Meanwhile, back inside the Spot, E.J. was concluding his dream. Isabel love said, "Well, are you going to tell us about your deliverance from witchcraft?"

E.J. started: "I was fifteen when I overheard my mother telling my dad he should go and get some help for himself. Well, he did, and when he came back from seeing the witch doctor, he relayed what she had told him. It seems she told my dad that my mom's best friend, who happened to be a Spirit-filled Christian woman, had come over one day and stole my father's underwear when my mother left her alone to go into the kitchen. After that, the witch smashed an egg, and it came out black. She said a very bad spell had been put on him, and it would cost his whole paycheck to remove the curse. Because he was a prosperous man and our family had a nice car and house, she was jealous of that.

"Well, the spell was reportedly broken, and my dad got his job back, and the trials lessened, so my mother and father took that as a victory. But it really wasn't, because my mother never trusted her best friend again, and it forever ruined their friendship—even though they worked in church together.

"It took me getting saved and becoming an evangelist to really get them back to a godly trust and relationship with each other. You see, witchcraft calls names and breaks friendships, as well as starts lies and deception ... all to get money.

"The worst part of witchcraft is when someone uses it as white magic. You see, there's white magic and black magic."

Keith asked, "So, what's the difference?"

"Well," E.J. continued, "white magic uses witchcraft to make someone love you and give you control over them, and black magic uses witchcraft to harm or destroy your opponent. You know, this is my second wife. My first wife ... , well, we were not saved, and what happened is this: After dating my first wife for over a year, she was going to break up with me for another guy. So, I went to a witch doctor to gain her love. A curse was put on her, and we were married just a few months later.

"Then, one weekend, we were coming home from a nightclub when my car was in an accident, and she was killed instantly." With this, E.J.'s head dropped, and it took him some moments to recover.

"A few years later, I gave my life to the Lord and received the gift, and in one of our services, the guest evangelist prophesied to me and said, 'You were married once out of the will of God. The other man was her real husband.'

"You see, witchcraft always ends up putting you out of the will and plan of God. Just look at what the book of Acts teaches:

> *And it came to pass, as we went to prayer, a certain damsel possessed with a spirit of divination met us, which brought her masters much gain by soothsaying.* Acts 16:16"

Lenora spoke up, "I can understand that. Everyone that I ever knew that got involved with that stuff died a horrible death or was brought to poverty."

E.J. nodded his head in agreement and continued, "And fear always gets a stronghold in their lives. Look at the story of the witch of Endor in the Bible. Divination is the path people choose when they don't want to wait on God or to seek His ways:

> *When Saul saw the camp of the Philistines, he was afraid and his heart trembled greatly. When Saul inquired of the LORD, the LORD did not answer him, either by dreams or by Urim or by prophets.*
> *Then Saul said to his servants, Seek for me a woman who is a medium, that I may go to her and inquire of her.*

And his servants said to him, Behold, there is a woman who is a medium at Endor. 1 Samuel 28:5-7, NASB

"The important things is: how did God feel about this?

And Samuel said, Hath the LORD as great delight in burnt offerings and sacrifices, as in obeying the voice of the LORD?
Behold, to obey is better than sacrifice, and to hearken than the fat of rams. For rebellion is as the sin of witchcraft, and stubbornness is as iniquity and idolatry. Because thou hast rejected the word of the LORD, He hath also rejected thee from being king.
1 Samuel 15:22-23"

At that moment, I looked back to Earth, and could see that the heat continued to increase. Judgment continued through the night with screams, the sizzling sound of people burning, and the terrible odor of death. Through all of this, the elect were sleeping peacefully.

CHAPTER 11

DAY 3—THE UNCLEAN SPIRIT

This day, after the Elect woke up, they looked at each other to see who had the dream for that day's judgment. Isabel Love shook her head in a somewhat regretful manner and, after looking at her brother Charles, said, "Well, I had a dream."

Looking at her, I could see that she was a very beautiful white lady, sexy, alluring and quick on her feet, with a lot of joy and laughter. She continued, "In a few minutes all the Earth is going to go black like never before."

Then I looked at Earth and saw Matthew 24:

Immediately after the tribulation of those days shall the sun be darkened, and the moon shall not give her light, and the stars shall fall from heaven, and the powers of the heavens shall be shaken: and then shall appear the sign of the Son of man in heaven: and then shall all the tribes of the earth mourn, and they shall see the Son of man coming in the clouds of heaven with power and great glory. And he shall send his angels with a great sound of a trumpet, and they shall gather together his elect from the four winds, from one end of heaven to the other. Matthew 24:29-31

Sure enough, the sun went out, just like a light switch being turned off, first in one quadrant, or corner, of the Earth, then in another quadrant and another ... until all four corners were dark. But it all happened within thirty seconds.

The darkness penetrated the whole world, and people could no longer see clearly what was in front of them. Then, suddenly, the crying turned to screaming, and the screaming turned to hoarseness. This was true throughout the world and in all languages.

Parents could not find their children, and, for their part,children were frantic. Everywhere you could hear babies crying and screaming. Thousands of people were dropping over in their tracks, dying from heart attacks and an incredible fear caused by the day's events.

An hour later, it happened: a low-pitched thundering sound started and kept rumbling. It was weird, to say the least. An hour later, there was a high-pitched whistling sound, as the stars from Heaven started falling to Earth. It was like bombs going off all over the place. These stars burned deep into the ground, and you only saw the smoke at first and heard the rumbling thunder sound in the sky.

The low-pitched thundering sound continued and never stopped. Lightning lit up the skies and momentarily displaced the darkness every now and then, but there was no rain, only more heat. This went on throughout the day and into the night, with no moonlight to be seen. One thing was certain: God was angry, and time was up. The whole world knew that by now.

At midnight, you could see fires starting everywhere. Before long, they rose two feet high, then five feet, then ten feet, then twenty feet into the air.

Meanwhile, back at the Spot, Isabel was telling her story. "You see how all Hell has broken loose on the third day. That's been the story of my life. I told you that I was into real estate, but the real deal is this: God delivered me from being a high class call girl."

Surprised, Officer Pendleton spoke up, "You were a prostitute?"

Isabel, visibly sucking it up, answered, "Yeah, yeah, that's what I was. And after getting saved, God had to purge me from an unclean spirit, or lifestyle.

"The unclean spirit can be found in these verses ..." She read from the Bible:

When the unclean spirit has gone out of a person, it passes through waterless places seeking rest, and finding none it says, I will return to my house from which I came. Luke 11:24

For he said unto him, Come out of the man, thou unclean spirit. Mark 5:8

Isabel continued, "You see, the unclean spirits are in sexual sins such as adultery, fornication, lesbianism, homosexuality, beasteology, child porn and other sex offenses. Let me tell you how this spirit came to me.

"When I was just twelve, my step-dad would come into my room at night and do things to me when everyone else was asleep or my mother was working late. He eventually started having sex with me, but I was afraid to tell anyone. His words are still clear in my mind. He said that if I told anyone he would hurt my mother and my little brother.

"After a while, he started giving me money after sex. He eventually started bringing his friends over to have sex with me and would give me some of the money they paid him for it. I tried, time after time, to run away, but there was nowhere for me to go. To avoid him and his friends, I would hang out at a store or sit in an all-night restaurant, but I eventually had to go home.

"My mother and I drifted apart. She was so in love and so busy working that she never caught on to what was happening. Finally, one night, when he came into my dark room, I knew I had to do something to end this nightmare.

"It was cold that night, and I could hear his familiar footsteps coming my way. My body was tensing up, and my heart was racing, as it always did. But this time was different. I was rehearsing in my mind a plan I had laid out and gone over many times. *'This time,'* I said to myself, *'I'm going to do it.'*

"He turned me over and, as usual, was very rough with me. He smelled like a dirty wet dog.

"After it was all over, I went into the kitchen to make him coffee and toast, as he always required. But this time I put in his coffee the poison I had been hiding for a long time. He screamed at me, 'Hurry up. I've got to go to work.' He was an insensitive and brutish man.

"After drinking the poisoned coffee, he pushed his way past me and went out the door. I could hear his truck starting and then roaring off down the street. I never saw him again. Later that night, someone told me that he had lost control of his truck and crashed into a gas station, and his truck had gone up in flames. Since nothing much was left of him, his death was ruled an accident.

"A year later, my mother was still taking his death hard. She was very depressed. One night she was in the living room in front of the fireplace just staring as if she were trying to decide something, and I dared to approach her with the truth. I thought that would liberate both her and me. I said, 'Mother, I need to talk to you.'

"She looked up at me and said, 'Have a seat, child.'

"I sat down beside her. She said, 'My child will be fifteen years old in a few days.'

"I smiled, 'Yes, Mother, I will be.'

"She said, 'My little girl will soon be a woman.'

"When she could see a frustrated look on my face, she said, 'What? What's wrong, child?'

"Now I was crying and said, 'Momma, I need to tell you something.'

" 'What?' she asked.

" 'It's about Mr. Ronnie, Mother,' I started and then wasn't sure how to tell the terrible truth. 'He ... He ...'

" 'What is, girl?' she demanded.

" 'Well, Mother,' I ventured, 'it started when I was thirteen.' Then I just blurted it out, 'He started raping me.'

"Mother looked terrified. 'What are you saying, Isabel?' she urged.

" 'Yes, Mother,' I continued, 'he raped me and said he would kill you and my little brother if I told you. He showed me a gun and told me all the people he had shot over the years. He said he would hurt you. And, even if I did tell you, he said, you wouldn't believe me anyway.'

"Now I was sobbing more and more violently. Mother grabbed me and held me in her arms to comfort me.

"But I wasn't finished with my confessions. 'That's not all, Mother.' I said.

"Mother looked shocked and quietly said, 'What else, child?'

"Now there was no turning back. I blurted out the rest. 'He started prostituting me with his friends and beating on me. It got so bad and went on so long that I couldn't bear it any longer. The last day I saw him, after raping me, he pushed me into the kitchen to make him some coffee. Well, Mother ... , I put poison in his coffee. That's why he lost control of the truck and crashed. It wasn't an accident, Mother. I killed him.'

"Up to that point, Mother was still holding me, but now she looked up into the air and then suddenly and violently pushed me away. She was in a rage and shouted, 'Get away from me, you lying, dirty little !>@#>@$. Get away, you little whore. How dare you taint Ronnie's name like that.' She was pushing me violently toward the door. Then she screamed at the top of her voice, 'Get Out! Get Out!' I ran out the door and never looked back. That's when I started my life as a prostitute. I was just fifteen, and my life was never the same again."

There was a momentary silence in the room, and then Jim Kaker asked, "So, what happened after that?"

Isabel continued, "Well, fifteen years later, I was on my way to meet a client ... well, a trick, when my car broke down right beside an old-fashioned tent revival. Man, those people were shouting and having a great time in there. I thought they must be crazy.

"I stood outside the tent listening, and in the preacher's message, it seemed like he was retelling my life. I was mesmerized and suddenly found myself under the tent. Actually two of the sisters had come over and invited me in, and I gave my life to the Lord Jesus and received the gift that night.

"Immediately I started a five-year search for my mother, praying that God would lead me to her. Miraculously, just as had happened with me, her car broke down next to a tent revival we were having.

"I was an usher that night, so, when I saw a woman outside, I went over to invite her in. She was crying and her head was down so that I could not see her face. But, as I got closer and she raised her head up, I got the surprise of my life.

"I stood there speechless, and when she realized who I was, her face lit up. Then we both stood speechless for a long moment, just staring at each other in disbelief. Finally, the silence was broken by a sister who was with me. Bewildered by our reaction, she asked, 'Do you two know each other?'

"My mother answered first, 'Yes. That's my child Izee.'

"The sister looked at me for a response and then suddenly remembered my testimony about my mother. Lovingly, she turned to me and asked, 'Is that her?'

"A million thoughts were racing through my mind from childhood until that moment, and I broke and cried, 'Yes,' and we fell into each other's arms.

"Mother hugged me tight, and we cried together. Later, after the brothers had fixed her flat, she asked me to sit inside her car and talk, and what she said blew my mind.

" 'Izee,' she began, 'I need you to know something.' I looked at her tentatively, not sure what was coming next. 'You did not kill your step-dad, Izee,' she said.

"I couldn't believe what I was hearing. 'What?' I asked, 'What are you saying, Mother?'

"She looked at me with all seriousness and said, 'It's like this, baby. Before your step-dad died, I had been in touch with your real father, and he told me what was then the talk of the town about Ronnie. In fact, that last night, I had called your father over to confront Ronnie, but he was in the very act with you. Your father, who, incidentally, passed just last year, was so angry about it that he rigged your step-dad's brakes and put a rattlesnake in his truck that night. Your step-dad rolled out of the truck before it crashed and blew up, but he actually died from multiple snake bites.'

"I was sobbing at this point, and Mother hugged me and we cried together. The next night she gave her life to the Lord and received the gift under the big-top tent."

"Wow! Wow! God is something else!" the rest of the group responded to this testimony.

Then E.J. said, "So, you were purged from an unclean spirit. That means judgment today is for those with unclean spirits."

"Yes," Isabel answered. "I'm afraid so. You got it!" Then I heard her voice-over as we went back to watch the continued purging of the Earth and the heavens. She was saying: "All those who haven't repented of their adultery, fornication and homosexuality, beasteology and pedophilia will die today. On Earth, the fires are burning everything in their wake. The flames are high in the sky, and many are trapped inside sink holes and are burning from the fires.

"It's everywhere. Now people are in the streets, running and screaming. The heat is unbearable and is overtaking them as the fire races over them to destroy them.

"The rumbling and thundering never stops. The only time you can see anything is when there is a lightning strike. The Earth is stinking with the smell of burning bodies. Houses are burning, buildings are burning, the White House is burning, and the Kremlin is burning in Moscow. The people in the Pentagon are hunkered down, even as it also burns."

Neon signs for gay activities were burning up. Gays by the thousands were burning, and they were on their knees looking up, begging God to forgive them, even as they burned to ashes. The gays, fornicators, adulterers and those into beasteology and pedophilia were all catching on fire and running. They were burning and running and dying.

Every so often, a flame of fire would strike many in their private parts first and then spread all over their bodies. It was an incredible scene, as they would try to use their flaming hands to put out the fire in their private parts. They were jumping into ponds, rivers, and lakes, but those were on fire as well.

One member of a gay couple was screaming at the other, saying, "I was in church doing right, and now look what you have done to me."

A lesbian couple was arguing. One of them said, "I thought the minister said we would go to Heaven. What is this? We were deceived." She screamed at the top of her voice as the fire engulfed her.

Some were falling into the huge sink holes that were opening up as the Earth heated up, and they were burned alive underground. I could hear a sound like an egg frying, as the ground opened up and swallowed them, and they burned. Lesbians, gays, adulterers and fornicators were all on their knees screaming and begging God to forgive them and confessing, "Jesus is Lord," but it was too late. I was reminded of the scripture that says:

> *For it is written, As I live, saith the Lord, every knee*
> *shall bow to me, and every tongue shall confess to God.*
> Romans 14:11

I heard many people now saying, "I should have listened to the preachers!"

Then I saw the politicians. They were crying out, "Oh, God! Oh, God! Jesus, please help us!" And many of them were also running and repenting.

At this point, all planes that had been flying around with nowhere to land were crashing and burning. There were the sounds of explosions all over the Earth.

Meanwhile, back at the Spot, Charles Cobbs was giving a testimony. "While we are on it, let me tell you about another unclean spirit. It's called gay, transvestite or trans-gender."

Raymond asked, "What's the difference? Gay is gay, isn't it?"

Charles Cobbs continued, "As our society grows and matures, so do our definitions. *Transsexual* is the medical term for a person who has changed their physical gender to their desired target gender. In my case, I changed my gender from male to female. Many females wish to become males. A transsexual lives full-time in their new gender and usually has had some sort of reassignment surgery, changing their physical appearance and/or taking hormone replacement.

"In the strictest sense, a transsexual is a person who has had surgery to change their physical appearance to match their target gender, and then they live full-time as this gender. Some transsexuals move into society and live solely as their target gender and identify as only male or only female.

Transgender is a more general term and has been widely accepted as politically correct, while the word *transsexual* has had a negative stigma associated with it. Maybe this is why I tend to call myself a 'transgendered woman' or, for short, a 'trans-woman.' *Transgender* can refer to any person who dabbles with the role opposite to their birth gender. This is the more common definition of transgender and the umbrella it covers.

"I am going to put both transvestites and cross-dressers together for simplicity. Transvestites and cross-dressers are typically heterosexual males who wear traditionally feminine clothing. A transvestite has been labeled in the past as associating cross-dressing with sexual arousal, but that term has now changed to *transvestic fetishism*. Cross-dressers don't associate with the LGBTQ community and don't see themselves as anything but straight/heterosexual drag queens and drag kings. They are even not usually labeled as cross-dressers or transvestites."

"Why?" someone asked.

"Good question, actually. People who dress in drag tend to be gay, and cross-dressers tend to be straight. As with all labels, nothing is black and white, and there are plenty of gray areas. One person might identify as transgender but not as transsexual, another as cross-dresser and not transvestite.

"There are also people who don't identify as any gender. They are gender queer and don't feel part of society's norms and the stereotypes associated with each gender. They like to think of themselves as 'gender queer' or 'gender free,' free from all gender labels and gender stereotypes, including clothes, roles and any other society gender conformity."

Officer Pendleton then asked, "So, what's your story? Were you a transgender person? Did you have an operation to change your gender to a women?"

Charles continued, "No, I was gay, but when I got saved I brought many transgender persons to the cross who had become women through surgery. When the Lord came into the lives of those transgender individuals and they truly repented of their sins, we taught them to live as eunuchs for the rest of their lives. You see, *'to whom much is given much is required.'* They altered God's design for themselves on Earth.

Jim Kaker spoke up, "When these people come to the Lord, can't doctors reverse the operation and make them a man again?"

At this point, Doctor Cheng butted in, "No, once a transgender operation has been performed, it cannot be reversed without serious debilitating consequences."

Charles said, "The doctor is right. That's why I chose to be a eunuch. It's really the best thing for someone in my position to do. Why, even straight gays sometimes make that commitment.

"But, to answer you, Mr. Kaker, being a male is a matter of birth, but being a man is a matter of choice. I chose to be a man of God. You see, when I was a child, my twenty-three-year-old mother would go out partying in clubs with her closest girlfriend, Nini, and other girl friends, often leaving me sleeping at Nini's mother's house. Although I was just a child of seven, Nini's seventeen-year-old brother Donald would come into the room where I was sleeping, take me to another room and have sex with me. He threatened to hurt me really bad if I told my mother. I was very afraid of this guy. I did tell his grandmother, but nothing was ever said or done.

"This cycle went on for two years and finally ended only when we moved out of the city. From that time on, I was in and out of homosexuality for a few years and was struggling with my feelings and the past experiences I kept under wrap. I was finally able to get victory over those feelings and the pain they caused when I gave my life to the Lord and started going to a Pentecostal church.

"Over time, I started visiting different churches when my church wasn't having any activities, and eventually went to a very high-profile church musical that I loved. I came back very excited about having met a national artist there, and I shared it with my pastor (who walked very strongly in the prophetic). He just looked at me as I was telling about the event, and then he warned me strongly to stay away from that ministry. I agreed, but only half-heartedly, letting the devil tell me that my pastor was just intimidated by that other church and the thought of losing me as a member. I should have known better because I had seen this man walk in a strongly committed relationship with the Lord and knew that he feared no one in the Spirit.

"I kept sneaking back over there and was eventually invited to an overnight gathering at the pastor's resort house.

We were told that leading city officials would be there, as well as musical artists and local athletes. This made me feel very special because I was a fairly shy person and was rather intimidated being around people I would normally see only on TV. So I went.

"At first, it seemed like a wonderful event, but as the night wore on, people started coming out with alcoholic drinks and later marijuana. This blew my mind, but I felt that I did not dare act square in front of all those important people. I mean, hey, I was a no-name singer at a little Pentecostal church, and these people could be my meal ticket to the top.

"Then, suddenly, the lights went dim, and the people started partnering up and having sex and crossing over with each other, men with men, and men with women. Everybody seemed to be changing up, so when a well-know guy grabbed me, I didn't resist. Even as I let go, however, I was crying out to Jesus on the inside to please forgive me. All I could think about was my dear pastor's voice saying, 'Don't go back there! Don't get caught up in that!'

"That next day was so bad! I was devastated. I cried all the way to work, I cried during lunch in my car, I cried going home, and I cried in my sleep. This went on for a few weeks until one day my pastor looked into my eyes while he was preaching and said, 'I don't see the glow you had before. What has happened?' Later that night I called him and told him all about it. He was very disappointed in me for not obeying the word he had given me, but he lovingly reached out to me, prayed for me and said to me, 'Never go over there again!'

"This time I listened and I got back on track ... only to discover a month later that I had contracted HIV during that orgy. 'Wow! Why, Lord?' I prayed, 'Why?' I had repented!

"I called my pastor, but I was crying so hard he had to urge me to get control of myself and then tell him what had happened. As soon as I could speak, I unloaded the bombshell news.

"My pastor was quiet for a few seconds and then I blurted out, 'Pastor, I need to expose those people!'

"He said, 'No! No! You don't want to do that! You might not live to tell the story. They may try to do something to you.'

"I said I didn't care, that I needed to get a release and maybe that would honor the Lord.

"He said, 'No! Get before God daily and get a committed prayer life, and in time maybe the Lord will release you to go to them privately and individually to forgive them and release them. That,' he said, 'would be far more effective. This news is not for the world to hear.' I thank God because years later I am saved and filled with His precious Holy Spirit and closer to God than ever before.

As we closed our eyes for the night, we saw and heard the destruction continuing on Earth and the rumbling and thundering sound that would not go away.

CHAPTER 12

DAY 4—THE SEDUCING SPIRIT

Early the next morning we woke up to the sound of horrible human suffering on Earth. Everything was burning or suffering from the heat and flames that got ever closer to those who were still alive. Some were dying slow deaths from burn wounds and heat exhaustion.

And there was nowhere to run. The fire or heat seemed to be coming from all sides. The whole Earth was one huge furnace. Even the wild animals were screaming as they slowly died agonizing deaths.

We saw pastors and other religious leaders with small and large ministries burning. They had missed the Heaven-bound train, and now they were on their knees, crying and repenting, begging Jesus to forgive them. In fact, leaders from all faiths were crying out and repenting, saying, "Jesus is Lord!"

I saw church signs burning up, and crosses on fire, falling off of church buildings. Political officials, famous athletes and the rich and famous were all crying like babies, realizing too late that they were in the furnace of God's affliction.

The thing that got me was the slow agonizing death that many were suffering, even from day one. It was as if God was allowing some to suffer, while others burned up instantly. The Bible calls this *the greater damnation."*

I saw Pastor Jim Kaker and his wife Laura waking up and talking with the elect. It was obvious, they said, what this day was. Officer Pendleton asked, "What is it?" The others were looking in anticipation for the answer.

Pastor Kaker responded, "Overnight I dreamed about the seducing spirit and how God is going to destroy ninety percent of the religious and Christian leaders and eighty percent of the Christian communities of this generation. Of course, all of the unsaved will be destroyed because of the seducing spirit.

"This spirit is described in First Timothy:

You see how the Spirit speaketh expressly, that in the latter times some shall depart from the faith, giving heed to seducing spirits, and doctrines of devils.
1 Timothy 4:1"

Pastor Jim continued, "The seducing spirit comes to lead us into false doctrines and the occult and to pollute the Gospel of Jesus Christ and lead us away from the Christian life of faith. It even causes us not to pray for and financially support the true works of our Lord Jesus. God delivered me and my wife from a seducing spirit years ago.

"It all started when I was a young evangelist and pastor. I was preaching the Gospel of Jesus Christ very boldly and faithfully. We saw slow growth and occasional miracles here and there. After a year or so, we had worked our little church up to a hundred or so members, and things were going well.

"We were all very innocent and excited. Then I went to attend a pastoral conference on church growth. The meeting was very different from the other conferences I had attended on this subject. The pastors all seemed to be very prosperous, as well as the speakers and the host. They all poked fun at hard-line 'fire and brimstone preachers' and laughed and made jokes about their ignorance in reaching this generation with a softer message of love and tolerance. I remember particularly one speaker who said: 'Look at me! Today I am a millionaire. The Lord has blessed me with cars, homes and a two-thousand-member church after I learned the truth and started teaching the new message, the true Gospel of Jesus Christ. Don't listen to these hellfire and condemnation preachers and that cross stuff. Follow the winners. Love the people and preach messages of hope.'

"As the meeting progressed, I met and made friends with a whole new group of pastors and ministers. Then, when I got back home, I changed my entire church structure and met with my leaders to give them the new rules for the church. Those who didn't agree were asked to re-sign or risk being fired."

Now Laura spoke up: "I thought Jim had lost his mind. Against my wishes and pleas, he even cut ties with old clergy friends who didn't agree with this new doctrine. Eventually the church (and our marriage) went through a serious change. The gifts and moving of the Spirit stopped."

With tired eyes, Laura continued, "The church grew, but so did the kind of sins that were happening among our members. Within two years, we already had five hundred members. It all happened so fast. But as we looked around, marriages were breaking up, and unrepentant sinners were in charge and abusing their powers. There was one leader, Jeremy, who went with several different women in the choir, and there were many unwed pregnancies. It was a mess. We had failed to protect the baby Christians, and our single moms were now left to the wolves.

"Meanwhile, to make matters worse, Jim had hired a gay musician who really was good on the organ, but he brought along many of his friends. It wasn't long before we were at eight hundred members, but many of them were openly gay.

"These people supported Jim and me with huge offer-ings, and our lifestyle changed significantly for the better. We were flying everywhere, buying the best of clothes, driving the best cars and living in a very luxurious home.

"This all came to a head one day when I tried to admon-ish the choir director about the way he was talking around a young teenage man, and he rudely rebuked me and told me to stay in my place. When I challenged him, he told me that he had built the choir, and if he left he would take all of the choir members with him and his gay friends would all leave. He boldly said that our lifestyle would go back to that of living in poverty.

"Shocked, I immediately called Jim and told him what had happened. Jim was quiet as I spoke to him, so I said, 'Jim, are you there?'

"Jim answered me, 'Sweetheart, I'm sorry about this, but don't worry. I will speak to Ronnie. Okay, honey?'

"Later that night, at home, Jim was looking confused and somewhat afraid. 'So, Laura,' he said, 'what's going on?' When I told him again what had happened, he said, 'Sweetheart, I need you to be very understanding here.'

"I said, 'Understanding? Ronnie disrespected me in front of several leaders. He has to be dealt with.'

"Jim looked sad and his head was down. Then, he said, 'Laura, what's up with you?' He looked into my eyes, and I could see that he was crying. In a very sorrowful, soft manner, he said, 'Honey, I need you to back off and don't be so controversial.'

" 'Controversial?' I said, 'he disrespected me. Are you going to stand up for me or what?'

"Jim answered, 'Baby, we don't need these problems right now. I am about to go on television and, if all goes well, I will soon be broadcasting worldwide. These folks are paying for all of that, so please back off!'

"I couldn't believe what I was hearing. I said, 'Jim, I stood by you when Jeremy defied you in front of the leaders, and I told you then to take a stand. Jeremy is a whoremonger, and he's gone to bed with several women in the church. Several members and even your leaders have come to you time and time again about this, and yet you have not yet taken action. Jim, this is not you. What has happened.'

"Jim was flinching, but he couldn't find the words to answer me. Now I really got hot under the collar. 'It's because he's the biggest tithe payer, isn't it?' I challenged. 'You won't sit him down. He's still up teaching classes, and you won't sit him down.'

"Now I was screaming, 'That's wrong, Jim! That's wrong! And God is not pleased with it.'

"Jim now grabbed me by the hand, and I took the opportunity to look at him and say, 'We didn't have these problems when you were taking a stand against sin and preaching the cross.'

"By this time, Jim was frustrated, and he shouted back at me, 'Well, where did it get us? Struggling financially. That's where it got us!'

" 'But we had peace,' I protested, 'and the presence of God in our services. You just didn't have the patience to wait on the Lord. If you want to stop it all, I'll call a meeting right now and dismiss them all, and we can start over. Just remember, our daughter Gloria is going to college next year. Think about her before you answer.'

"I didn't know what else to say, and when Jim didn't seem to respond to my words, I looked into our daughter's bedroom and then, with my head down, I threw my hands into the air and gestured *Just forget it*!

"As I was walking away, Jim said, 'I knew you would see it my way.' So both Jim and I compromised the Gospel in order to grow the church. Churches put a lot of words and tags on it, but the bottom line is that all ministers who are not teaching or preaching the uncompromised Gospel of Jesus Christ and all Christians who are not obeying the Word of God are being seduced by the seducing spirit."

Laura now began to weep as she continued the story. "One month later my ... our daughter got caught up with the wrong crowd in church and went out with Deacon Jeremy's son and his friends. The teens, instead of going to the movies, as they had said, snuck off to a party where the guys got drunk. As they were leaving, someone insisted that my daughter or one of the other young ladies drive home. Jeremy resisted this idea and said that no one was going to drive his daddy's car home but him. He assured everyone that he was not drunk.

"After making a stop to pick up one of the girl's babies from the baby sitter, Jeremy began speeding down the road, clowning behind the wheel and causing my daughter to fuss about his driving. Then, as he tried to pass another vehicle on the roadway, a tractor trailer hit them head on, and they were all killed instantly. The impact was so hard it threw the baby through the air, and it landed nearly fifty yards away in a field."

This was obviously a very emotional subject for her, and she took her time composing herself to be able to continue. "Jim was never the same after that. He no longer prayed with the gift. He started drinking and would come home drunk even after his Sunday morning sermons. When our marriage began to fall apart, Jim was asked to step down for a year and seek treatment.

"With unpaid bills mounting up and daily arguments, I felt hollow inside. There was nothing there, nothing for Jim, nothing for the church and even nothing for me. I soon found myself in bed with Deacon Jeremy, who had stood by my side throughout the whole ordeal. Our common loss had drawn us together. He was hurting for his son, and I was hurting for my daughter. Of course, my husband was hurting too. He was hurting for the church, for me, for our daughter and for God.

"Eight months passed and one day, while sitting on the little porch of our humble home, Jim had the radio on and heard about a prophetic evangelist who was preaching each night at a little church not far from us. He got up and said, 'Let's go!' I hurriedly got ready. Having not been to church for eight months I was very lonely and really missed the good old days when Jim and I had been busy for Jesus.

"We made our way into the revival that was fiery hot and Pentecostal in nature. The crowd was only about fifty people and they were mixed between Blacks, Whites and Hispanics. The evangelist himself was Black and was preaching right at us. His sermon was tailored for us about churches and people that have compromised God's Word to build gods of mortar and brick. He emphasized how there will be a famine for the Word in the end and shared how blessed we really are and don't know it. He preached boldly, saying it's not by power nor by might, but by the Spirit that must we live, preach and get blessed by God.

"Jim and I began to break and, at the end, when the altar music kicked in, we made our way down front. When we got up to the altar, the preacher was prophesying to folks. He looked at us and called out: 'Preacher, you two have lost much in the last year, even a loved one, but God says to tell you they are in Heaven. They repented at the last moment.'

" 'And,' he continued, 'God said to tell you that this time around, where you failed before, you won't fail anymore.' Jim and I could not take any more. We both ran and fell into the preacher's arms and wept and praised God.

"After that year of restriction was up, the deacons paid us a visit, to bring Jim and me back. But both Jim and I shared with them that our message and vision had changed, and we would definitely not be going back there. Instead, we started Faith Center Church, and three years later we were at five hundred members. This time, there was no compromise. The preaching of the cross and living free from sin were back, and we now enjoyed a strong presence of the Lord in our marriage, in our ministries and in our daily living. There's really nothing in the world like the peace and power of God and the gift operating in your life and ministry."

Then I heard Keith say, "So, a seducing spirit is like a whorish woman, seducing a good man."

Pastor Kaker answered, "Yes, but it's more than that. It operates on Sundays in church when it's time to give into the Lord's work. The seducing spirit tells us not to give because our bills are due. 'You are going to go under if you do that,' he says. 'You are stupid! You are just making the preacher rich!' And on and on it goes. Satan's job is to stop the Kingdom from advancing because the advance of God's Kingdom means the destruction of his kingdom. It's that simple."

Isabel Love, speaking in her high-class, flirtacious voice, now interjected, "It's so true. That makes so much sense to me. Let us remember what the Bible says:

As we have therefore opportunity, let us do good unto all men, especially unto them who are of the household of faith. Galatians 6:10

For the scripture saith, thou shalt not muzzle the ox that treadeth out the corn. And, The labourer is worthy of his reward. 1 Timothy 5:18

CHAPTER 13

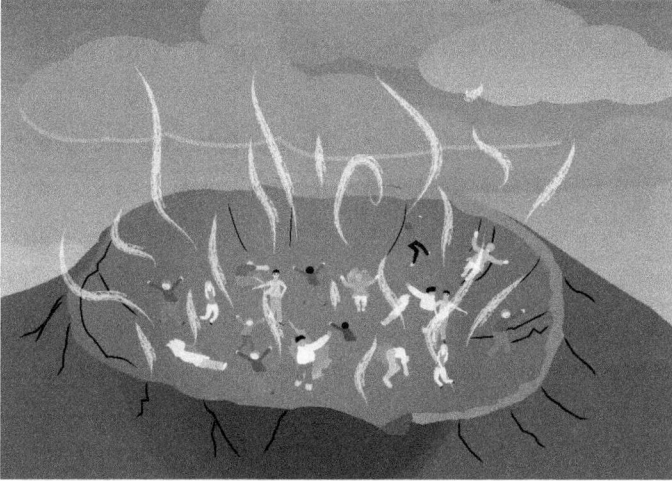

DAY 5—THE SPIRIT OF FEAR

Day 5 was no different. We all woke up to the fearful events taking place on the Earth—the ongoing low-key rumbling, with occasional loud thunder claps, and the sounds of bodies burning in a dark furnace. The only time people could see each other was when the occasional lightning would light up the skies.

It was dark, stars were falling, and the people had nowhere to run but into each other. There were screams all over the world, people begging God to forgive them and saying loudly, "Jesus is Lord!"

I remember hearing a Black grandmother saying, "Oh, Lord, please have mercy." Thousands were saying it. "Have mercy, Lord! Have mercy, Lord! Please, Lord! Mercy! Mercy!"

And then there were the cars blowing up, tankers blowing up, bridges crumbling and skyscrapers crashing. Dogs and other animals were screaming, and military tanks, submarines and ships were exploding. Nuclear fallout was spreading, and people were running and losing body parts as they ran.

One lady was running on fire when half of her right leg fell off. Next half of her leg fell off. She fell down and was trying to keep moving like a dog on all fours. But then her body crashed to the ground, smoking like charcoal.

When the lightning clapped, you could see all over the world. I saw eyes wide open in dying and dead, burned bodies!

Meanwhile, back at the Spot, Doctor Mei Li Cheng was speaking. "Well, guys," she said, "It's my day!" The others were shaking their heads in agreement, now knowing the pattern.

Isabel Love said, "Well, what's your story?"

Doctor Cheng began, "The Lord delivered me from a spirit of fear, which is what this day of destruction and purging is all about."

Even as she spoke, they could hear the never-ending rumbling in the clouds and the screams, crying and moaning of those left on Earth.

Then E.J. Oday said, "The Bible says:

For God hath not given us the spirit of fear; but of power, and of love, and of a sound mind.   2 Timothy 1:7

Raymond Ortiz said, "You know, fear is probably one of the worst of all demonic spirits. It causes people to do bad things to each other."

"Like what?" Isabel Love asked.

"For starters," Doctor Cheng offered, "there are several nations, including America, that have operated toward certain races from the spirit of greed or fear. You see, out of fear, people become greedy and become fearful of losing their wealth. Many times they became ungodly in the process.

"Look at the Mexicans and the Black race today. Those two groups were very much a part of our early American culture, and yet, look where the Blacks are today. They have the highest crime rate, the highest rate of incarceration, the highest murder rate for twenty-five years and under and the highest divorce rate. A Black woman is the least likely to be married among all races, and most Black homes are led by a single mother.

"Among the Black race, why is it that the women have all of the opportunities and jobs rather than the men? We must ask ourselves why this is."

Charles Praxton now spoke up, "But look how far we have come in America. I mean, look, we've now had a Black president, and we have Black legislators, Black mayors and city officials and on and on."

Pastor Kaker added, "But that's not what God was after. If we had a heart change, America (and maybe even the world) would have been a better place. As White Americans, have we ever really accepted Blacks and Hispanics as real people, equal to us? Much of our 'progress' has been about being politically correct, not real change. We tore Black families up, raped them and/or made slaves of them and then forced them to accept this as normal behavior. Afterward, we never really mentored them like we should have been doing all along. Every race came to this country intact except theirs."

E.J. Oday added, "Excuse me, pastor, but I must say something here."

Pastor Kaker nodded his head okay, and E.J. continued. "I've seen and heard a lot of blame over the years about slavery and this, that and the other. But if the truth were to be told, Blacks and Jews were first known as the original Hebrew Israelites and were given a chance to live blessed by God. But, because of their disobedience, they were allowed to suffer in slavery and lost their original heritage, as seen in Deuteronomy. It says:

And it shall come to pass, if thou shalt hearken diligently unto the voice of the Lord *thy God, to observe and to do all his commandments which I command thee this day, that the* Lord *thy God will set thee on high above all nations of the earth: referred!*

Deuteronomy 28:1

"What Blacks must do now is come back to God and break the curse they put themselves under. God has promised either blessings or cursings. We have to choose. First, let's look at the promised blessings:

And it shall come to pass, if thou shalt hearken diligently unto the voice of the Lord *thy God, to observe and to do all his commandments which I command thee this day, that the* Lord *thy God will set thee on high above all nations of the earth: and all these blessings shall come on thee, and overtake thee, if thou shalt hearken unto the voice of the LORD thy God.*

Blessed shalt thou be in the city, and blessed shalt thou be in the field.

Blessed shall be the fruit of thy body, and the fruit of thy ground, and the fruit of thy cattle, the increase of thy kine, and the flocks of thy sheep.

Blessed shall be thy basket and thy store.

Blessed shalt thou be when thou comest in, and blessed shalt thou be when thou goest out.

The LORD shall cause thine enemies that rise up against thee to be smitten before thy face: they shall come out against thee one way, and flee before thee seven ways.

The LORD shall command the blessing upon thee in thy storehouses, and in all that thou settest thine hand unto; and he shall bless thee in the land which the LORD thy God giveth thee.

The LORD shall establish thee an holy people unto himself, as he hath sworn unto thee, if thou shalt keep the commandments of the LORD thy God, and walk in his ways.

And all people of the earth shall see that thou art called by the name of the LORD; and they shall be afraid of thee.

And the LORD shall make thee plenteous in goods, in the fruit of thy body, and in the fruit of thy cattle, and in the fruit of thy ground, in the land which the LORD sware unto thy fathers to give thee.

The LORD shall open unto thee his good treasure, the heaven to give the rain unto thy land in his season, and to bless all the work of thine hand: and thou shalt

*lend unto many nations, and thou shalt not borrow.
And the* LORD *shall make thee the head, and not the
tail; and thou shalt be above only, and thou shalt not be
beneath; if that thou hearken unto the commandments
of the* LORD *thy God, which I command thee this day,
to observe and to do them: and thou shalt not go aside
from any of the words which I command thee this day,
to the right hand, or to the left, to go after other gods
to serve them.*   Deuteronomy 28:1-14

"Now, let's look at the curses God declared for people
who are disobedient:

*But it shall come to pass, if thou wilt not hearken unto
the voice of the* LORD *thy God, to observe to do all his
commandments and his statutes which I command
thee this day; that all these curses shall come upon
thee, and overtake thee:
Cursed shalt thou be in the city, and cursed shalt thou
be in the field.
Cursed shall be thy basket and thy store.
Cursed shall be the fruit of thy body, and the fruit of
thy land, the increase of thy kine, and the flocks of
thy sheep.
Cursed shalt thou be when thou comest in, and cursed
shalt thou be when thou goest out.
The* LORD *shall send upon thee cursing, vexation,
and rebuke, in all that thou settest thine hand unto
for to do, until thou be destroyed, and until thou perish quickly; because of the wickedness of thy doings,
whereby thou hast forsaken me.*

The LORD shall make the pestilence cleave unto thee, until he have consumed thee from off the land, whither thou goest to possess it.

The LORD shall smite thee with a consumption, and with a fever, and with an inflammation, and with an extreme burning, and with the sword, and with blasting, and with mildew; and they shall pursue thee until thou perish.

And thy heaven that is over thy head shall be brass, and the earth that is under thee shall be iron.

The LORD shall make the rain of thy land powder and dust: from heaven shall it come down upon thee, until thou be destroyed.

The LORD shall cause thee to be smitten before thine enemies: thou shalt go out one way against them, and flee seven ways before them: and shalt be removed into all the kingdoms of the earth.

And thy carcase shall be meat unto all fowls of the air, and unto the beasts of the earth, and no man shall fray them away.

The LORD will smite thee with the botch of Egypt, and with the emerods, and with the scab, and with the itch, whereof thou canst not be healed.

The LORD shall smite thee with madness, and blindness, and astonishment of heart:

And thou shalt grope at noonday, as the blind gropeth in darkness, and thou shalt not prosper in thy ways: and thou shalt be only oppressed and spoiled evermore, and no man shall save thee.

Thou shalt betroth a wife, and another man shall lie with her: thou shalt build an house, and thou shalt not dwell therein: thou shalt plant a vineyard, and shalt not gather the grapes thereof.

Thine ox shall be slain before thine eyes, and thou shalt not eat thereof: thine ass shall be violently taken away from before thy face, and shall not be restored to thee: thy sheep shall be given unto thine enemies, and thou shalt have none to rescue them.

Thy sons and thy daughters shall be given unto another people, and thine eyes shall look, and fail with longing for them all the day long; and there shall be no might in thine hand.

The fruit of thy land, and all thy labours, shall a nation which thou knowest not eat up; and thou shalt be only oppressed and crushed always.

So that thou shalt be mad for the sight of thine eyes which thou shalt see.

The LORD shall smite thee in the knees, and in the legs, with a sore botch that cannot be healed, from the sole of thy foot unto the top of thy head.

The LORD shall bring thee, and thy king which thou shalt set over thee, unto a nation which neither thou nor thy fathers have known; and there shalt thou serve other gods, wood and stone.

And thou shalt become an astonishment, a proverb, and a byword, among all nations whither the LORD shall lead thee.

Thou shalt carry much seed out into the field, and shalt gather but little in; for the locust shall consume it.

Thou shalt plant vineyards, and dress them, but shalt neither drink of the wine, nor gather the grapes; for the worms shall eat them.

Thou shalt have olive trees throughout all thy coasts, but thou shalt not anoint thyself with the oil; for thine olive shall cast his fruit.

Thou shalt beget sons and daughters, but thou shalt not enjoy them; for they shall go into captivity.

All thy trees and fruit of thy land shall the locust consume.

The stranger that is within thee shall get up above thee very high; and thou shalt come down very low. 4 He shall lend to thee, and thou shalt not lend to him: he shall be the head, and thou shalt be the tail.

Moreover all these curses shall come upon thee, and shall pursue thee, and overtake thee, till thou be destroyed; because thou hearkenedst not unto the voice of the LORD thy God, to keep his commandments and his statutes which he commanded thee.

And they shall be upon thee for a sign and for a wonder, and upon thy seed for ever.

Because thou serve not the LORD thy God with joyfulness, and with gladness of heart, for the abundance of all things;

Therefore shalt thou serve thine enemies which the LORD shall send against thee, in hunger, and in thirst, and in nakedness, and in want of all things: and he shall put a yoke of iron upon thy neck, until he have destroyed thee.

The LORD shall bring a nation against thee from far, from the end of the earth, as swift as the eagle flieth; a nation whose tongue thou shalt not understand; a nation of fierce countenance, which shall not regard the person of the old, nor shew favour to the young: and he shall eat the fruit of thy cattle, and the fruit of thy land, until thou be destroyed: which also shall not leave thee either corn, wine, or oil, or the increase of thy kine, or flocks of thy sheep, until he have destroyed thee.   Deuteronomy 28:15-51

E.J. continued, "So, you see, the Black American seed is really that of God's chosen people, and only Black America can turn this around."

Pastor Kaker added, "Yes, and we've gotta understand that from the Jews to Spanish Americans, the Vietnamese, Indians and Chinese, they all came to America with strong families and relationships in place, all except the Blacks."

He now looked at his wife who had teared up. She walked over to him, took his hand, and the two of them looked back in time. She said, "Black America, we are so sorry for what has happened to you and your families, the dreams of owning your own home, raising a happy family, walking in the park with your wife and achieving your dream for life, walking with your head high and not secretly feeling like a loser or second-class citizen deep down inside.

"Black women, because your men are battling shame, you are battling fear, and, for that, we're sorry. We understand that every woman needs security. It's the joy and pride of life.

"Every woman needs to be able to lie down at night and feel safety for her children and not live on the edge, worrying that at any moment bad news of some tragedy will come by way of a phone call. Every woman deserves to live out her dream with the man of her dreams whom she loves and respects. What would have happened if all of the businesses and corporations of the nation would have said, 'Let's forgive our Black brothers for their criminal past. Come and go to work for us. We forgive your past. We forgive your past! It's time for a second chance.' "

Now Brenda spoke: "As a child, I would be so afraid when Daddy wasn't home. So many nights I lay fearful, not being able to go to sleep. Some nights I would wet the bed because I was so afraid. But, then, when Daddy came home, everything was okay.

"To the Mexican community, you helped to build this nation. You worked for slave wages and did the work of two and sometimes three men and were paid less than half what the lowest-paid American received. Until 2014, you led the labor force. Still, your race has the lowest educational achievement level in comparison to other immigrants, and we're sorry for that. Our education system has failed you!"

They all looked remorseful and saddened. Then their eyes locked on each other and they looked at Officer Pendleton and his wife Brenda and at Lenora and her friend Raymond.

Now E.J. spoke again, "Well, there is more to the spirit of fear than that." All heads turned toward him.

Isabel said, "Explain it, Big Boy!"

Jim said, "I agree."

E.J. continued: "America and the American people are controlled by fear. We were raised to operate in fear. Look at our political process, how over the years even we Christians became afraid to speak out for Jesus and for God's Word. We have given in to abortion and homosexuality because of social and political backlash, fear of losing our jobs, or being exposed in the liberal media—which have really pushed their liberal agenda, and it has taken control of America.

"Businesses gave in for fear of losing business, and preachers gave in for fear of losing their tax exemption for taking a political stand."

"Well," Doctor Mei Li Cheng added, "if I could, I would like to add another insight to the fear—if you will bear with me. The Word of God says:

There is no fear in love; but perfect love casteth out fear: because fear hath torment. He that feareth is not made perfect in love.   1 John 4:18-20

"So many of my patients today, even the believers, are battling with mental issues and challenges like clinical depression and medical issues caused by fear. That's why the Word says that God has given us a sound mind. You see, I believe that fear comes to attack your mind, to cause you to doubt God's Word and give into man's word or the doctor's word."

E.J. added, "Yeah, there's nothing worse than a wishy-washy Christian. One day you believe God, and the next day you are cursing and doubting Him."

Raymond chimed in, "I call them 'lookie-loous'. They come to church looking, but they have never really bought into the faith."

"Personally," Mei Li Cheng said, "I have a story to tell. I was raised in a home where my father hated people of other races. You see, life was not always easy for our family. When we came to America from Taiwan, we were all very nervous.

"Some months after arriving in America, my dad and step-mother were in a store shopping, and I was in the car relaxing and listening to music, when, out of nowhere, two Chinese thugs approached the car and put a gun in my face. One of the guys was small and thin, and the other was taller and bigger.

"The two men pulled me out of the car, threw me into a van and sped off. They took me to several teller machines and forced me to withdraw money. Then, when they were satisfied that there was no more money to extort, they took me to a park and were about to rape and murder me. I remember being slapped and threatened, with a gun to my head, and told that if I said a word they would kill me. I just knew I was going to die.

"Then, suddenly, out of nowhere, a Black man appeared and came to my rescue. He jumped out of a truck and came upon the scene with a shotgun and pumped it. Click! Click! The two robbers dropped their guns to the ground.

"The Black man shouted, 'Let her live, man! Let her make it!' The two rapist were startled and threw their hands in the air, dropping their weapons as he approached. He told them, 'Move! Outrun your feet!' and they jumped in their van and sped off.

"I looked down and saw their guns still lying on the ground. My hero saw them as well. Bending over, he picked them up and held them out for me to see better. 'Fake suckers with fake guns,' he said. 'These are just for play.' And he threw them into the air.

"He then came over to me and calmed me down, for I was sobbing and about to go into hysterics. As I cried in his arms, I realized there was something special about this man. Fast forward to a year later, and my hero and I were married. As it happened, he turned out to be a well-known businessman. He prayed with us often, and I totally received the gift.

"God knows what is in our hearts and minds. Just the day before the robbery I had made my mind up to do a very evil thing to my stepmother. Back in Taiwan, my dad and stepmother had been financially blessed and I grew up sheltered. But I was very afraid of people and never had many female friends or meaningful relationship with the opposite sex, all because of fear.

"But I hated my step-mother. I mean, it was a known fact, by all of my brothers and sisters, that our stepmother had not only broken up our father and mother, but she was heavily into witchcraft and controlled Dad like a puppy. Growing up, she always kept us isolated and spoke negatively of any friends we ever had.

"When I got married, the Lord dealt with me through my husband concerning fear. I've learned that fear can really mess up your life. The Bible says that *"God has not given us the spirit of fear but of power, of love and a sound mind."* I did not have a sound mind. I was always so indecisive, I always read too much into any little thing that happened to me. I trusted no one and thought my friends were always lying or against me and drilled them all the time over any little issue. This made my friends a little uncomfortable to be around me.

"Fear, the Bible says, *"has torment"* and can lead into serving false gods, witchcraft, jealousy, envy and strife. Galatians 5:20 shows that strife can keep one from entering into the Kingdom of Heaven. Strife, however, is found in many families and in churches, and this has kept Christians from walking in the full blessings of God. Strife causes many not to see the power of God and not to experience total healing in their lives. Proverbs says that God hates those who sow discord among the believers.

"Just look around at the world today. News media are causing strife, our families are in strife, on our jobs there's strife, and even in the church we can't seem to get along. I now understand what the Scriptures meant when they say:

Nevertheless when the Son of man cometh, shall he find faith on the earth?　　　　Luke 18:8

And because iniquity shall abound, the love of many shall wax cold.　　　　Matthew 24:12

"In the last days the love of many shall wax cold."

With that thought, the elect retired for the night. But, first, they all got down on their knees together and prayed.

CHAPTER 14

DAY 6—THE DEAF AND DUMB SPIRIT

On Day 6, the group awakened to the silence of total darkness all over the Earth. All nations were mourning around the world, and people were screaming in every language.

There were no stars, no moon and no sun. The low-sounding rumbling was still there. As the lightning flashed, you could see human suffering all over. There were children running in the streets, and a pregnant lady, crying and holding her stomach.

You could see Chinese, African, French, Russian, Middle Eastern and Muslim populations, including terrorists, all burning and screaming. In their own languages they were saying, "Oh, God! Oh, God! Help us, Jesus!"

People were jumping into any pool they could find, but in most cases, pools, lakes and rivers had now burned dry. There was no water anywhere, and people were hungry, thirsty and dying from the burns and the smothering heat. If God had destroyed the world by water, it would have been much better than this.

Airports, military bases and hospitals had all crumbled and were burning. We watched as one tall hospital building began to cave in floor by floor, the walls buckling from the heat, until the entire building fell in a smoky heap.

The sizzling sound of the streets melting and popping like firecrackers was terrible. There were animals burning. Whole herds of cows were stampeding to nowhere, and people continued running and burning and dying.

The White House, the Kremlin and every other headquarters of world power had crumbled into a heap like so much garbage. In the rubble, dead presidents and the bodies of their staff members smoldered from the fire before crumbling into ashes.

Lenora now read a passage of scripture:

Seeing they do not see, hearing they do not hear and do not understand.   Matthew 13:14

"There was no perception," Lenora continued, "no knowing. A mind-blinding spirit kept them from salvation:

In whom the god of this world hath blinded the minds of them which believe not, lest the light of the glorious

gospel of Christ, who is the image of God, should shine
unto them.   2 Corinthians 4:4

"This mind-blinding spirit affected both unbelievers and believers, causing darkness, a lack of illumination and a resulting hardness of heart toward God. It resulted in a willful rebellion, an obstinate unbelief and a refusal to believe God. Satan then had the power to blind their minds and thoughts."

Laura added, "So we can understand why the Lord said the Gospel must be preached in every nation, so that men and women can call on Jesus and be saved. Those who have rejected Him can call on Him even while they are being burned alive."

"Yes," Raymond said, "you are so right. If people would only have only listened to the Word and just done what it said! But, no, they were stubborn and turned their eyes and ears away from the truth. God calls it a deaf and dumb spirit."

Laura said, "Most people think this spirit only attacks the physically deaf and dumb, but it goes deeper than that. You see, there are many in my church who got saved through sign language. But, more so, this spirit keeps people from even wanting to hear the Gospel." She looked at Pastor Jim Kaker and said, "Today, God is destroying those who have this rebellious spirit."

Laura added, "Pastor, I believe the Lord has told you to share something with us."

Now in tears, Pastor Kaker said, "Yes, Laura," but then he hesitated.

E.J. spoke up and said, "Well, what, Pastor? What is it?"

Pastor Kaker, still teared up, said, "You know, the Lord filled us with His precious Holy Ghost, and yet we, at times, have been ashamed of Him.

"For example, we let the world laugh at our Pentecostal, Charismatic and religious experiences, and this caused us to quench the Holy Spirit. We quit dancing in the Spirit, shouting, praising and ministering in the Spirit. We allowed ourselves to become intellectual so that we could gain those with money, power and prestige to our churches, but you can't change the Word of God. In Acts 1:8, it says:

> But ye shall receive power, after that the Holy Ghost
> is come upon you: and ye shall be witnesses unto me
> both in Jerusalem, and in all Judaea, and in Samaria,
> and unto the uttermost part of the earth.

"We receive power only after the Holy Ghost comes upon us or into our lives. Then God said, in Mark 16:17:

> And these signs shall follow them that believe; ... they
> shall speak with new tongues.

"This is what took place on the Day of Pentecost. The Bible says the disciples of Jesus, those who loved Him and wanted to do His will, were gathered together in one place when it suddenly happened:

> And when the day of Pentecost was fully come, they
> were all with one accord in one place. And suddenly
> there came a sound from heaven as of a rushing mighty
> wind, and it filled all the house where they were sit-
> ting. And there appeared unto them cloven tongues

like as of fire, and it sat upon each of them. And they were all filled with the Holy Ghost, and began to speak with other tongues, as the Spirit gave them utterance. Acts 2:1-4

"You see, the Holy Spirit was their way out. The Bible says that He will lead and guide us and also comfort us:

Howbeit when he, the Spirit of truth, is come, he will guide you into all truth: for he shall not speak of himself; but whatsoever he shall hear, that shall he speak: and he will shew you things to come. John 16:13

But the Comforter, which is the Holy Ghost, whom the Father will send in my name, he shall teach you all things, and bring all things to your remembrance, whatsoever I have said unto you. John 14:26

But when the Comforter is come, whom I will send unto you from the Father, even the Spirit of truth, which proceedeth from the Father, he shall testify of me. John 15:26

Nevertheless I tell you the truth; It is expedient for you that I go away: for if I go not away, the Comforter will not come unto you; but if I depart, I will send him unto you. John 16:7

"Yes, it happened just as God promised:

The God of our fathers raised up Jesus, whom ye slew and hanged on a tree. Him hath God exalted with his right hand to be a Prince and a Saviour, for to give repentance to Israel, and forgiveness of sins. And we are his witnesses of these things; and so is also the Holy Ghost, whom God hath given to them that obey him. Acts 5:30-32

"The best part may have been that this Holy Ghost power was free for all who sought it. All they had to do was obey God's Word."

Laura then spoke: "Let me see if I can't make it a little more plain. We need to understand that many believers missed God in their businesses, marriages and careers because of not walking in the Spirit. I believe the number one goal of every believer should be to learn the voice of God and walk in the Spirit. God has said that if we walk in the Spirit we will not fulfill the lusts of the flesh:

This I say then, Walk in the Spirit, and ye shall not fulfill the lust of the flesh. Galatians 5:16

"You see, I had a very stubborn heart and a rebellious spirit and attitude toward God. Even though I became a believer, I still often wanted to do my own thing. So many times God's Spirit would be pulling on my heart to do a certain thing or go to a certain place, and I refused."

"I can identify with that," Lenora said. "Years ago I was an intern at the television station, and there I met a man named Ron, who was a production assistant. We were immediately attracted to each other and, after seeking the Lord, we decided to get married. (Ron truly was a strong Christian believer.)"

Then Lenora looked down rather sadly and began to share how a man named Harold had come into her life one day after her mother had visited the station to see her. Harold was a producer and he was very successful and financially set and had been with the station for years. "That day my mom met Harold as she was walking down the hallway, and he accidentally bumped into her. 'Ma'am,' he said in his polite and ingratiating way, 'may I help you? Are you here to see someone?' Mom replied that she was there to see me, and Harold (who had been eyeing me for some time), took it from there.

"Later, as my mother was leaving, Harold just happened to be leaving as well. (I always believed he planned it that way!) Anyway Mom said goodbye to him and noticed that he got into his new Mercedes-Benz. From that day forward, she never stopped talking about him and pushing me to marry him. I was twenty-one and still living at home with her, and she took advantage of the fact that we had a lot of time together.

"In time, Mom convinced me that this man would make a far better mate for me than Ron, and I will never forget the night at dinner when I broke the sad news to Ron that our engagement was off. It hurt him so badly.

"Ron said, 'You are only doing this because of your mother. I know you love me.' I will never forget the tears in his eyes as he said, 'Laura, I'm not going to lie on God and say "God said you are my wife," but I will say that His Word says, *"He that finds a wife finds a good thing and obtains favor from the Lord!"* I don't believe that God commands two people to marry, but I do believe that He confirms two people in a marriage!'

"Grabbing me and holding me gently, he said, 'Baby, I feel so much peace about this, and I know God will bless us. I know you deserve the best of the best, the fine car, new house and a lifestyle that requires a lot of finances, but what I don't have in finances, I have in favor, God's favor.' "

Sadly, I stubbornly resisted what was in my heart and married Harold. I was happy for about a month until the real Harold came out. Pretty soon he started running around on me, gambling, drinking and the works. After five years of marriage, we had lost everything—our cars and our home. Harold had gotten fired from his job, and we were all but homeless. Then, trying to maintain his high lifestyle, Harold got caught up in a criminal pyramid scheme, and is now serving twenty years of federal time.

After my divorce, I started going back to church again, trying to put my life back together. Then one Monday I ran into Ron at the Post Office. He was looking very good and appeared to be successful. He told me that he had recently purchased his own TV network. After making some more small talk, we walked out to his car, and that was when Ron told me about his wife and introduced me to her.

This announcement came out of left field and caught me by surprise. Ron and his wife had become rich. She was driving a Porsche Panamera, and he was in a brand-new, top-of-the-line Mercedes!

To make a long story short, Ron and his wife hired me on the spot, and I've been working for them ever since. Ron had never given up on God or his dreams of being a broad-caster. I'd had a chance to be his partner in life, but I didn't listen to the right voice and the clear teachings of the Word of God. It was my loss.

CHAPTER 15

DAY 7: THE INFIRMITY SPIRIT

The group was waking up to the all-too-familiar sound of constant low-grade thundering that would not quit. Brenda was looking out of the building, but then she glanced into the monitor and looked rather nervous.

Officer Kendleton, her husband, looked at her and said, "Honey, what is it? Then, sympathizing with her, he continued, "It's your day, isn't it, Honey? It's your time?"

"Yes," Brenda answered, tearing up.

She got control of her emotions and continued, "I will be the first to say that not every sickness or disability is a demon. Sometimes we battle things because of the results of fallen mankind, of not using wisdom, or of eating things we know are harmful to us."

Isabel Love chimed in, "Sweetheart, you just need to come out with it. Come on! Now, what is it you are trying to tell us?

Dr. Cheng said, "Brenda, it's all right. Take your time."

"Well," managed Brenda, "today God is cleansing the Earth of infirmities or those people who did not repent of the sins that brought on their disability or disease."

At this point, E.J. calmly interjected, "In Luke 13:11, the Bible speaks of a woman who had been crippled for eighteen years and was healed by Jesus on the Sabbath day. Luke said that she had a spirit of infirmity, basically a disabling spirit. The New International Version says that she was *'crippled by a spirit.'* Simply put, a demon caused the woman to be crippled for eighteen years."

"Well," Brenda continued, "many years ago, at the early age of eight, I went blind and started battling emotional challenges. My parents took me to all types of medical specialists, but no one had any answers. At the age of sixteen, while on my way to school one morning, I felt nauseated and had the handicapped bus turn around and take me back home.

"After feeling around the door lock, I finally found the keyhole, put the key in, and made my way inside. The bell that normally rang when anyone entered the house was broken and, therefore, did not make any sound. I didn't give that a thought. I didn't want to disturb my mother on her day off from work, so I went straight to my bedroom, lay down and went to sleep.

"About thirty minutes later I was awakened by the sound of a man talking and my mother laughing. I quietly made my way to the living room door and put my ear against it so that I could hear better, and I was shocked by what I heard. The man I had heard talking was apparently my mother's lover, and they were enjoying themselves in a sexual way. I stood there in shock, feeling sorry mostly for my hard-working father who was at work that day. I cringed at the very thought. How could my mother do this to our family and to my dad? How could she sneak around and cheat on him like this?

"But nothing in the world could have prepared me for what I was about to hear next. As I continued to listen, the man said, 'How is my child doing?'

"My mother said, 'Brenda's fine.'

"They talked about one day telling me who my real father was. This so shocked me that I let out a loud sigh, and then stood there gasping for breathe. Frozen with fear and anger, I could not move.

"Suddenly they stopped talking, and I could hear my mother saying, 'Be quiet! I heard something.'

"I heard footsteps coming my way and was able to move quickly toward and into a hallway closet. I knew by instinct where it was because it had been my playhouse for years. Mom and the man both came through that door and looked all around, but seeing nothing, they eventually closed it and went back inside.

"It was two years before I had the courage to confront my mothers about all of this. It was a cold day in January, and Mom and I were in the car headed to a clothing store. There would be a church cell group meeting at our house on Sunday night, and I needed a new dress.

"About that time, Mom and Dad (I still loved him and called him Dad ever after knowing that he was not really my father), were having some difficult moments with their marriage. They were both going to church now, but still the strife in our home had reached an all-time high.

Something freed me and, as Mom pulled up at the store to park, I told her about the day I had overheard her with her lover in our house. She didn't respond until I said I knew he was my dad.

" 'Mother, how could you?' I asked. I could hear her sigh of relief as she began to try to explain the whole sordid affair. But I wasn't about to receive it. I threw my hands in the air in frustration and then jumped out of the car, grabbed my walking cane, and began feeling my way to the store.

"The next evening in the home-fellowship service our pastor spoke. The worship and singing had touched me in a special way that night, but it was the pastor's words on forgiveness that really spoke to my heart. At the close of the service that night, the whole group prayed for me. Then I met with the pastor and gave my life to the Lord. I confessed all that had happened to me, as well as my mother's secret.

"The pastor stayed over, after everyone else had left that night and counseled with the three of us. He shared from Galatians:

But if ye be led of the Spirit, ye are not under the law. Now the works of the flesh are manifest, which are these; Adultery, fornication, uncleanness, lasciviousness, idolatry, witchcraft, hatred, variance, emulations, wrath, strife, seditions, heresies, envyings, murders, drunkenness, revellings, and such like: of the which I tell you before, as I have also told you in time past, that they which do such things shall not inherit the kingdom of God.

But the fruit of the Spirit is love, joy, peace, longsuffering, gentleness, goodness, faith, meekness, temperance: against such there is no law. And they that are Christ's have crucified the flesh with the affections and lusts. Galatians 5:18-24

"Then, the pastor looked directly at my mother and waited to see what her response would be. She dropped her head and began to confess everything to my dad (who was now my step-dad). Immediately after that, I felt my right eye jump, and then my left eye jumped.

"A warm feeling came over me, and suddenly I received the Gift. I started seeing a shadow and cried out.

"The pastor said, 'What is it, my dear?'

" 'I can see,' I said, 'I can see! It's my eyes! I can see!' I was speaking in tongues and praising God.

"Looking at what was happening to me, my step-dad broke down and wept. I stood very still, not knowing what his next reaction might be. Then suddenly he turned to Mom and said, 'I forgive you!'

"He stretched his hands out, not only toward her, but also toward me, and I will never forget his words: 'Some men have custodial children that they never receive, but today God has given me a daughter out of the love of His heart.' We never discussed the subject again! It was forever forgiven and forgotten.

"The point is that I want you see how the blindness never left me until I had forgiven my mother and she had repented. Later, when talking with the pastor, we committed ourselves to attend Sunday night house meetings in the homes of several of my best friends that had issues and infirmities, and the same kinds of miracles happened there."

Pastor Kaker then said, "That's very understandable. That's the way God works."

Brenda added, "Yes, take for instance my friend Tony. According to medical doctors, Tony would be confined to a wheelchair for the rest of his life. When I was blind, Tony would share some very intimate things with me about his past.

"Tony's parents were very well off and ran a very successful restaurant. Over the years Tony would ride along with them as they made their rounds collecting from clients. So he knew they had a lot of money and he knew where it was kept. Many times, according to Tony, he would sneak in the back of the restaurant and steal money from the money drawers, leaving his parents to think an employee had stolen it. This sometimes resulted in an employee being fired. It happened several times over the years, he said.

"Tony always talked about one particular Spanish-speaking lady. She was a single mother with four children and was trying her best to raise them on her own. One day, when she was on duty at the restaurant during a busy holiday, Tony went in and stole $3,000.00 from the till to party with his girlfriend and her friends. As a result, charges were filed against the young mother, and she was convicted and sentenced to four years in prison. Still, Tony never came forward to confess that he was the one who had stolen the money. The last time I knew, the young lady was still doing time for his crime.

"But, thank the Lord, after we had a Bible study at his parents' house, Tony was convicted and received the gift.

Later that night he shared with his parents everything he had been doing. The very next day, on Monday morning, Tony's doctor called to tell his parents that there was a new procedure that could very well help Tony walk again.

"Tony had the procedure, and some weeks later, he was beginning to learn to walk again. And, by the way, the young lady was released from prison, and Tony's parents gave her a big check and offered to restore her to her managerial position."

Now Isabel Love spoke, "So, is it right to say that diseases such as cancer, diabetes, etc. are all part of a curse from God or they come because of a particular act of sin?"

Brenda answered, "Well, Miss Love, let me tell you this: maybe not all diseases, but for sure some.

"And here's a case in point: One Sunday we had a home meeting at the house of my friend Teresa Hartford. Teresa's dad was also there. At the end of the service, Mr. Hartford came over for prayer and received the gift. There was so much joy and peace, as we all celebrated this joyous occasion that always brings total peace into one's life.

"Mr. Hartford was battling the last stages of terminal cancer, but right in front of everyone he got on the phone and begin calling several women to set up meetings with them. It turned out that Mr. Hartford had forced these women to give him sexual favors in return for keeping their jobs under his supervision. He now met with each of them and got down on his knees and personally repented. Amazingly, during Mr. Hartford's very next hospital visit, test showed that his cancer had gone into remission.

"You see, the Bible says that after the Holy Ghost comes, a person shall have power. This is not only the power to cast out demons from others, but it is power to be loosed from the demons in us. That power, to be honest, is power to confront your own personal fears, your own wrong actions and your own wrong lifestyles, as well as the power to repent and get things straight in your life."

Isabel Love added, "One thing I never did understand was why so many believers who really seemed sold out to the love of God suffered so much."

Pastor Jim Kaker answered this difficult question, "You know, the Word says that as Christ suffered in the flesh, so we must also suffer, in order to crucify our flesh. Let us remember that the fiery trial that is to try us is not to harm us but to help us to be more like Jesus and to get us back on track in life.

"Let me tell you a little story: There was a young man years ago who worked in a shoe store, but he heard about a big job opening at the train station. He called in to work one day and lied to get off so that he could put an application in for the other job. On the application for the new job, he also lied about his experience. He eventually got the job, as a conductor on a passenger train, but it required him to work out of town for at least the first year.

"The problem was that the young man was married and had been having some issues with his wife. They had seemed to be working things out through counseling, but now that he was on the road all the time, one day he received divorce papers.

"Frustrated by this, he now spent his time at work emotionally upset, and soon enough he forgot to give the proper orders, and his train went down the wrong track and crashed into a herd of cows, killing many of them, and then hit a gasoline tanker truck that had stalled on the tracks, causing a huge explosion.

"Amazingly, the young conductor was so lost in his own hurting world that he didn't even notice these things. When it was finally brought to his attention, he came to himself and began praying. Realizing the train was going the wrong way, he now got it under control.

"After the train had stopped, he went and met with the passengers, confessing his failure to them and explaining why he had been so preoccupied. He knew that his confession would surely cost him his job, but he asked them to forgive him nevertheless.

"Now the question was should they get the train turned around? Or should they go on in the direction they had been traveling? There was no consensus among the passengers. Some had important commitments and wanted the train to continue on its present course. Others insisted that it should turn back.

"The assistant conductor had been sleeping through all of this and now he was awakened and asked his opinion on what should be done. He was adamant that the train continue on its current course and quickly.

"The repentant conductor announced that anyone wishing to go the other way could get off with him. They would walk back far enough to get another train that was due to come along in a few hours. About twenty percent of the people got off to go with him. The rest continued on.

"After walking for only about ten minutes back down the track, the group on foot heard a loud bang and saw the light of an explosion. Next came the sound of train cars crashing down the mountainside. It seems that the train that didn't turn back soon ran out of track and plunged down a cliff.

"Now, I ask you: In the eyes of God, was that conductor responsible for the deaths of the passengers who stayed on the train? I say, no, for he repented and was forgiven. But going back to the point where the conductor got off track in life, we must conclude that it started with the lie that had been told a year before on his first job. That lie caused his divorce because he was no longer able to go to the counseling sessions needed to heal his marriage. It is, therefore, safe to conclude that he never should have been a conductor in the first place. Why do I say that? Because he had to sin, to lie, to get the job.

"Also, let us remember that hurting people hurt other people. It is not intentional, but it happens. Look at the fiery trial God had to allow that conductor to go through to get his life back on track."

To this, Brenda said, "That's very good, Pastor Jim, but my reasoning for saints suffering or not obtaining God's best is simple. It goes back to the Scriptures:

You shall love the LORD your God with all your heart and with all your soul and with all your might.
Deuteronomy 6:5, NASB

And He said to him,
You shall love the Lord your God with all your Heart,
and with all your soul,
And With All Your Mind. Matthew 22:37, NASB

"Far too many people are loving God only halfheartedly."

The group shook their heads in agreement. The thunder roared as they listened and watched the burning and screaming souls who had gotten off the purging and saving path of God!

Part Part V

The Final Judgment

CHAPTER 16

THE JUDGMENT FOR ABOMINATIONS

And that was the last day of the world as we know it. As it had done continuously for the last several days, the lightning flashed for seconds every fifteen minutes or so and gave a glimpse of what was left. Between flashes, the world was as dark as ever, so dark you could not see anything in front of you, behind you or on the side of you.

Pastor Jim spoke, "You know the Bible says (and we have preached it all along), that God will judge abominations. His great anger is mentioned fully one hundred and forty-two times in the King James Version of the Bible."

Officer Pendleton said, "Wow!"

Isabel Love agreed, "I never knew that!"

Keith Bakerson said, "Yes, that's right. Most of those times it was used to state the great anger God has for homosexuality, lesbianism, the killing of innocent babies and other unnatural acts."

At this point, the tall fires were subsiding all over the world, but in their wake, dead, tarred bodies lay smoldering everywhere, and you could hear the whimpering of those still alive.

The ashes of the dead were flying in the air, and buildings had been reduced to ashes, as had stadiums, streets and even entire mountains.

The rumbling that had been constant for the last seven days had now stopped. All the stars, the moon and the sun—all the formerly visible heavenly bodies—were gone.

The whole Earth smelled like death and burning sulfur, and the smoke of it was gaging people and causing extreme coughing everywhere. The Earth had truly become the furnace of God's judgement.

The only people left suffering now were those whom God had considered to be the greatest sinners. They were the ones who had openly defied His ways. They had poked fun at Him and His Word and stood in direct opposition to everything He stood for. They were the coworkers of Antichrist, and with them, were the adults who committed sexual sins with animals and children and those who had abortions and those who performed them. At the top of the list, however, were those who had entered into gay marriages and activist and politicians who had pushed that particular agenda to change history.

The whole world, including America, looked like a war zone, with the last survivors barely moving. Those who were left at this point were crawling on their bellies and sliding along on their backs, using any part of the body that was not yet burned and desperately trying to find some place of comfort. Every remaining person was moaning, sobbing, crying or screaming. All you could see of their burnt bodies were their white eyes. Yes, the eyes of these men and woman around the world, looking up, told the story.

Then, suddenly, it was as if God was finished, and the thunder stopped. The rumbling stopped, and all became very quiet. It seemed as if God had quieted everything so that those who were left could hear their own moaning.

Some, thinking that it was all over and they had survived it, felt a momentary hope. Many of them began to worship God, begging Him to send Jesus again to give them another chance. Many were crying and begging Jesus to save them. All else was quiet.

Then, suddenly, the skies lit up with silver, then red and finally black. Then, just as suddenly, a powerful-sounding voice came through the clouds and said: "Now, you will hear Me!"

All eyes were suddenly looking up, and many were thinking that maybe there was hope after all.

The voice continued, "I Am God, the Creator of Mankind. I gave you My Son Jesus, and you rejected Him. Your desire for sodomy and sexual gratification was stronger than your desire for spiritual dedication. You worshipped the god Molech by killing unborn babies, and for that, you worshippers of Molech and you Sodomites must die the slower death. For I AM THE CREATOR OF ALL MANKIND!"

The final words that roared around the world and shook the skies and the foundation of the Earth were these: "I AM ALPHA AND OMEGA, THE BEGINNING AND THE END!"

Then, suddenly, the thunder roared very loud and its clap shook the whole Earth, and, as it did, fire rose up three feet high and ten times hotter than ever. The resulting screams were gut-wrenching. One man screamed so hard his tongue flew out of his mouth.

Darkness came back, but we could hear bones crunching and the sound of a huge oven, and now the screams got louder than all other screams. All over the world people were in torment, screaming and crying out. Some were asking why they had not been warned. All were bowing, calling on Jesus, confirming the scripture that declares:

That at the name of Jesus every knee should bow, of things in heaven, and things in earth, and things under the earth; and that every tongue should confess that Jesus Christ is Lord, to the glory of God the Father. Philippians 2:10-11

It was happening before our very eyes. Angels and saints were bowing in Heaven, and evil men were bowing on Earth. Under the Earth, demons were burning to death and men and women in Hell were screaming in the flames.

At one point, the fire stopped, but this only increased the pain, as the damned shook and trembled in Hell from their horrible burns. And the reprieve, such as it proved to be, was only momentary. Within moments, the flames had returned, and the wicked were burned all over again. The resulting screams were unforgettable.

Then the thunder in the skyless atmospheres clapped for the last time. The only ones who would escape this fire were those who had overcame God's purging in the furnace of affliction. He said:

Behold, I have refined thee, but not with silver; I have chosen thee in the furnace of affliction. Isaiah 10:48

CHAPTER 17

THE NEXT GREAT AWAKENING!

GOD'S FINAL WARNING TO THE WHITE, BLACK AND ETHNIC CHURCHES OF AMERICA!

When I got to this point in the book, I thought it was done. Then one day, while meditating on God's Word and the book, God said to me, "You have not finished your book!"

I immediately asked Him, "Lord, what is it?"

He said, "I am very displeased with many churches in America and the believers in those churches."

I knew what He meant, for I have also been ashamed of many of our Black churches recently. For the next couple of weeks I listened carefully to what the Lord was saying to me, and He led me into some truths and some history that most of us have either overlooked or taken for granted.

The first thing the Lord showed me is that Christians have always made a difference in the world around them, but their influence was often silenced by the secular outcry of the day. Take, for instance, the early Abolitionist Movement to stop slavery. I read the following in *The Reader's Companion to American History*:

*Radical abolitionism was partly fueled by the reli-
gious fervor of the Second Great Awakening, which
prompted many people to advocate for emancipation on religious grounds. Abolitionist ideas became
increasingly prominent in northern churches and
politics beginning in the 1830s, which contributed
to the regional animosity between North and South,
leading up to the Civil War.*

*Although abolitionist feelings had been strong dur-
ing the American Revolution and in the Upper South
during the 1820s, the Abolitionist Movement did not
evolve into a militant crusade until the 1830s. In the
previous decade, as much of the North underwent
the social disruption associated with the spread of
manufacturing and commerce, powerful evangelical
religious movements arose to impart spiritual direction to society.*

*By stressing the moral imperative to end sinful
practices and each person's responsibility to uphold
God's will in society, preachers like Lyman Beecher,
Nathaniel Taylor and Charles G. Finney, in what came
to be called the Second Great Awakening, led massive
religious revivals in the 1820s that gave a major im-
petus to the later emergence of Abolitionism as well
as to such other reforming crusades as Temperance,
Pacifism and Women's Rights.*

*By the early 1830s, Theodore D. Weld, William Lloyd
Garrison, Arthur and Lewis Tappan and Elazar
Wright, Jr., all spiritually nourished by revivalism,
had taken up the cause of "immediate emancipation."* [1]

1. Eric Fonner and John A. Garratt, Editors, Houghton Mifflin Harcourt
    Publishing: 1991

I read that what really pushed the country into civil war was not only the efforts of Black people like Fredrick Douglas and Harriet Tubman, but also non-blacks like John Brown and preachers like Charles Finney. History shows that during a time when the people of both North and South knew slavery was wrong, it was still taboo to touch on the subject or talk about how wrong it was. But God used White men like Charles Finney, who preached powerful sermons about the sins of slavery and an unjust criminal justice system, to convert many in the North, and these then took up the banner to free slaves.

William Lloyd Garrison was one of those men. He was so touched by Finney's preaching that he started *The Liberator* newspaper that then played a vital role in getting information to the North about the horrors the southern slaves were going through. Garrison would forever radicalize the movement in the 1830s by forming the American Anti-Slavery Society. Through *The Liberator* he called for immediate and universal emancipation. Female abolitionists Elizabeth Cady Stanton and Lucretia Mott went on to become prominent figures in the Women's Rights Movement.

These early movements combined in the rise of an evangelical movement of Protestants from all backgrounds: Baptists, Pentecostals, Holiness people, Methodists, Presbyterians, Lutherans and others came together, and this brought on the Second Great Awakening. God showed me that the Civil War would never have been fought had it not been for these men and women of God.

Hat's off to the Quakers, as history has confirmed to us that they were the only believers who stood firm from day one against slavery and slave trading of the Indians and

Blacks. Much later in history, God sent Dr. Martin Luther King, Jr. with a mission to bring freedom by love and peace, and today, once again, God is looking for a unity revival among His people.

God told me He is angry with the church because we have allowed politics and the world to turn us against each other. Just as it was taboo or, at the very least, unpopular to speak out against slavery back in the 1800s, nowadays we face the same taboos when trying to unite believers to stand against the evils of our times. This includes evils such as abortion and homosexuality, just two of the many evils that are adversely affecting our nation. It is again taboo for Blacks to unite behind their spiritual leaders for godly reasons.

The Lord revealed to me that the Black Christian mothers and maids who took care of White children in a former time empowered those children with Christian values. It was those maids who counseled the children through to adulthood. It was not shocking at all, therefore, that those same young White children, now adults, turned out in record numbers to elect Barack Obama as the first Black President of the United States. Hats off to all those Black Christian mothers and maids who labored for Jesus and shared His love unselfishly, and hats off to all the White Americans who raised their children to love all people.

I especially want to thank my mother, the late Betty Barkley, who was one of those Christian maids who taught us to respect and love all people, that no one is better than another, that all people bleed red blood, hurt the same, need each other and need Jesus. I never once heard my mother utter a racist remark.

My heart ached for the Black ministers who went to a meeting just to pray with then Candidate Donald

Trump during his presidential bid. It seems that after the prayer meeting, those ministers were confronted by a very well-known Black television talk-show host. When they subsequently appeared on his show, he tore them to shreds, almost making them look stupid and, particularly, uninformed about the quest of Black people in America for equal rights. I thank God that most of those men, even though they did not seem to have their Masters in Black History, certainly had a Masters in the Love of God and the Unity of the Faith.

God's Word tells us to pray for unity in the Spirit. Too many Blacks have sold God out for the sake of their own Blackness. They are bitter and angry and have rejected God's Word and His way, replacing Him with Blackness. I have some minister friends who will not attempt to unite with White Evangelicals or diverse groups of Pentecostals or Southern Baptists, believing that they are all racists. But these are the same evangelicals or their offspring who helped Blacks gain their freedom years ago.

There are Black leaders today who would rather side with the gay and abortion movements which God's Word clearly shows grieve the Holy Spirit. While I can certainly understand their emotions (because I have experienced the evils of racism myself), as a Christian, like Paul, I must put those things behind me and *"press toward the mark of the high calling of God"*:

I press toward the mark for the prize of the high calling of God in Christ Jesus. Philippians 3:14

To many Blacks, Dr. King's message of peaceable protest seemed crazy and weak, but spiritually it was bold and full of faith. However, today God is not calling for freedom, but for the unity of His children. The Black minister who will dare to stand up and go against the grain by seeking unity with White, Hispanic and Asian Christian leaders, will be the new Finney or the new Dr. King who will usher in the next, and what could be, the final awakening. God is seeking those who will stand up for truth, start praying for a move of God in the nation, and start working together with President Trump and other government officials to bring it about. Only then will God's power began to penetrate the core of evil and stop the most deceptive movement in our nation today, none other than the Gay/Homosexual agenda that refuses to be satisfied or quiet.

Those who promote this wicked agenda are on a relentless quest for sexual gratification in all forms, with no restrictions concerning sexual partners. They even want our children, and they are demanding a total takeover of the American lifestyle. This agenda is, in part, inspired by the teachings of Saul Alinski, a community activist, whose 1971 book, *Rules for Radicals: A Pragmatic Primer for Realistic Radicals,* tells how to successfully run a movement for change by destroying America's values and godly culture. His angry rhetoric has fueled much of the anger, violence, division and hatred we see in America today. By using Alinski's techniques, the Gay Movement has all but taken over Hollywood and the motion picture industry. This takeover will soon be revealed in a huge scandal.

THE NEXT GREAT MOVE OF GOD

God's people should be focused on revival. God has something to say about it:

I, the Lord God, will send this revival as a revival of choice. Like Adam and Eve in the Garden of Eden, it is your choice. If you choose so, I will shorten the days of suffering even more for the elect's sake and will add more to the Kingdom, even after those numbered for the Kingdom have been met. The time is at hand, and I can come at any moment now. Be ready!

A very powerful wind will sweep across America and the world in the days ahead. This awakening will happen when unity comes forth from the Body of Christ, when diverse Christian races come together and begin to help each other. There will be a sharing of goods, as all saints decide to have all things in common. They will share food, clothing, cars and even their homes. Saints of diverse backgrounds will not only worship together; they will also live together.

Believers will help each other with legal, financial and social justice needs and the ills of the time. Pastors will begin to share their pulpits with those of other races and will begin interracial fellowships. Together, these saints will raise up against the evils of this generation and will see mighty signs and wonders follow them. They will experience joy and victory, while others are suffering agony and defeat.

Many who reject the Holy Spirit and refuse to be broken by the Spirit of Jesus will be exposed, and they will suffer many unnecessary pains and sorrows and be known as Victims of Satan instead of Victors Over Satan! God's Word admonishes us:

Endeavouring to keep the unity of the Spirit in the bond of peace. There is one body, and one Spirit, even as ye are called in one hope of your calling; one Lord, one faith, one baptism, one God and Father of all, who is above all, and through all, and in you all.

But unto every one of us is given grace according to the measure of the gift of Christ. Wherefore he saith, When he ascended up on high, he led captivity captive, and gave gifts unto men. (Now that he ascended, what is it but that he also descended first into the lower parts of the earth? He that descended is the same also that ascended up far above all heavens, that he might fill all things.)

And he gave some, apostles; and some, prophets; and some, evangelists; and some, pastors and teachers; for the perfecting of the saints, for the work of the ministry, for the edifying of the body of Christ: till we all come in the unity of the faith, and of the knowledge of the Son of God, unto a perfect man, unto the measure of the stature of the fullness of Christ.

Ephesians 4:3-13

MY DREAM CONCERNING HURRICANE HARVEY

For June of 2016 and, again, for January of 2017, if you go to my Facebook page and view my video post or purchase the Hope Sounds DVD, you can view my prophecy of Hurricane Harvey ravaging the Houston area. I saw in a dream that the city was surround by a high wall of water. That wall of water stood still. It did not move or flood the city. It was just standing there.

But there were tanks in the streets, and people were crying for President Trump to please come. I walked out to a soldier I saw on a tank and ask him if he could help me locate my church families. He told me that I would have to go back inside but that my family would be okay.

THE ACTUAL EVENT

Hurricane Harvey made history as the costliest tropical cyclone on record, surpassing the record set by Hurricane Katrina, and is the second costliest natural disaster worldwide (only coming behind the 2011 Japan earthquake and tsunami). After knocking the city of Houston to its knees with never-seen-before catastrophic flooding, the hurricane finally pushed on out of the city.

With half the city flooded and chaos still reigning, two more hurricanes formed in the Atlantic, posing a second and possibly a third threat. You could sense the fear and concern coming from Houston's news media and weathermen, knowing that if the next hurricane that was already in the gulf would hit us, it could very well totally devastate the entire city and its surrounding areas.

I will never forget seeing our mayor, Sylvester Turner, calling the whole city of Houston to prayer. Very soon after that, the weathermen began to smile, reporting a cold front that was sitting over Houston, blocking the path of the second and third hurricanes from coming our way. I could sense the Spirit of God saying to me that because the people were praying and unifying, He would not allow the other two hurricanes to come into Houston.

But, just as sure as I heard God say that, I also heard Him say that in the future, He would allow catastrophic events, with two and three calamities back to back, in order to draw people to Himself and get them to do His will!

Amen!

A PRAYER FOR SALVATION

For those of you who don't know Jesus as your Lord and Savior, please say this prayer:

Dear Lord Jesus,

I confess that You are the risen Son of God, You died on the cross for the pardoning of my sins, You are risen from the dead, and now You sit at the right hand of the Father to intercede for me. I ask You to forgive me of all my sins and come into my heart, fill me with Your precious Holy Spirit and become my Lord and Savior. Lord, I thank You for hearing my prayers. In Jesus' name, I am saved! I will now tell others that I am saved.

Amen!

My Name _____

Today's Date _____

To share your testimony on our broadcast or in our next movie, go to our website:

www.RedSea2CCN.com

Click on the upload menu and follow the prompts to send your testimony to us.

A PRAYER FOR THE SAVED

For those of you who already know the Lord, please say this prayer:

Lord Jesus,

Your Word says:

Purge me with hyssop, and I shall be clean: wash me, and I shall be whiter than snow.

Psalm 51:7

I ask You to cleanse me from all manner of sin and addictions. Cleanse me from anger, envy, jealousy, strife, fear and evil thoughts or worldly actions and thinking. Show me how to love my neighbor, my friends and my family and how to forgive those who have hurt me. And, Lord, finally, show me how to love You, even while You are purging me.

AMEN!

GET INVOLVED WITH "THE LAST SEVEN DAYS" MOVIE PRODUCTION AND REACH THE NATIONS

1. Go to: www.tbarthesound.com and click on the Last Seven Days Movie Menu. Sign up for the production team, acting roles or cooking and specialty teams to help make this movie the most life-changing of all times.

2. Purchase the DVD or USB entitled "The Hope Sounds of His Coming," with videos containing real-life testimonies from Dr. Tommie's prophetic ministry, as well as miracle events and the sounds of God speaking and bringing miraculous deliverances in churches and to individual people all over the world, plus special, never-before-heard prophecy of the changing lifestyles in America and how to survive in the days ahead.

AUTHOR'S CONTACT PAGE

You may contact the author in any of the following ways:

WWW.TBARTHESOUND.COM

email: tbsstudios@gmail.com

Phone: 832-476-9644 ext.5

Tommie Barkley
TBAR STUDIOS
P.O. Box 841563
Pearland, TX 77584

www.ingramcontent.com/pod-product-compliance
Lightning Source LLC
LaVergne TN
LVHW051235080426
835513LV00016B/1604